MW00628259

12 AMAZING FRANCHISE OPPORTUNITIES

— Second Edition —

Praise for the first edition of

12 Amazing Franchise Opportunities

"John Hayes's 12 Amazing Franchise Opportunities provides crucial and critical information for those who aspire to fame and fortune in the wonderful world of franchising. He knows and expresses clearly and coherently- most- if not all- of the many nuances there are in franchising. This is a must read for those who are already franchisors and franchisees, but especially for those who aspire to become successful as either."

William B. Cherkasky, former President
International Franchise Association
Former Executive Director
U.S Senate Committee on Small Business

"Dr. Hayes has an amazing ability to uncomplicated the franchise buying process. He's able to provide invaluable insight in the entire selection and purchase process. Dr. Hayes provides a road map. Which simplifies what would otherwise be a difficult and confusing process."

Tom Portesy, President
MFV Expositions

"It was through my involvement with International Franchise Association that I came to know and respect John Hayes, author of this book. John has been a featured lecturer at many IFA events, both from the perspective of the franchisor and the franchisee. He is an acknowledged industry expert. I have listened to his advice and if you are thinking about investing I a franchise, you should, too."

Gary Goranson
Founder and former CEO of Tidy Car
Founder and owner of WorkEnders, Inc.
Coach and creator of www.HouseCleaningBiz101.com

ii

"Dr. John Hayes is the world's leading authority on franchising. I know him as a franchisor, and when thinking about franchising our company he was my first call. You shouldn't make a franchise decision without reading everything Dr. Hayes has written on franchising.

J. Barry Watts, CEO
WealthCare Investment Advisors

"John's book is a must read for all prospective franchisees around the world. Most importantly, one must ask whether he/she has the personality, resources and commitment to work with the franchisor to achieve the desired success."

Albert Kong (CFE, CMC, Senior PMC)
Chairman/CEO
Asiawide Franchise Consultants Pte Ltd

"This is a fascinating book about a wide variety of franchising opportunities. If you want a road map to a new life in business, this is the book you must read!"

Mary Ellen Sheets, founder
Two Men & A Truck

"John Hayes is without question one of the world's foremost authorities on the subject of franchising and one of the most prolific and pertinent authors in this field. Congratulations on yet another informative and valuable resource book!"

Chris M. Levano, President
Quality Restaurant Consulting, Ltd.

"This one book should be read by every single franchise company and every single entrepreneur thinking of buying a franchise.... Everything this man writes or speaks I implement into my practice."

Mike Cheves, CEO
Hurricane Group, Inc.

"Coming from a thirty-year franchise veteran, 12 Amazing Franchise Opportunities for 2015, is one of the most profound and insightful publications I have ever read."

John L. Barry, President/CEO
Franchise Sales International

"John Hayes's 12 Amazing Franchise Opportunities 2015 serves as not only a primer for those interested in launching their own business, but also as an idea book that underscores the variety of opportunities that exist for wannabe business owners. A mobile dentistry repair unit? It's working and making money for franchisees. Hayes explains the concept of that and 11 other franchises that are waiting to come to your town. Spending a weekend with this book might just change your life."

*Richard J. Farrell
Journalist/Columnist*

"Excellent, and to the point book! John is the consummate franchise expert and teacher. If you're serious about becoming a franchise business owner, then use this book as your guidebook to the best franchising opportunity available today."

*Bill Porter, Executive Vice President
Access Brand Management*

Other best-selling books by

John P. Hayes, Ph.D.

Buy 'Hot' Franchises Without Getting Burned

101 Questions to Ask Before You Invest in a Franchise

Take the Fear Out of Franchising

7 Dirty Little Secrets of Franchising

Start Small Finish Big

Mooney: Life of the World's Master Carver

Network Marketing for Dummies
(with Zig Ziglar)

James A. Michener: A Biography

You Can't Teach a Kid to Ride a Bike at a Seminar
(with David Sandler)

12 AMAZING FRANCHISE OPPORTUNITIES

— Second Edition —

Compiled by

Dr. John P. Hayes

12 Amazing Franchise Opportunities, second edition

E-Book ISBN: 978-0-9997391-0-5

Paperback ISBN: 978-0-9997391-1-2

BizCom Press
1400 Preston Road, #305
Plano, TX 75093
www.BizComPress.com

Read this Disclaimer

Please note: Neither this book, its author, or its publisher provide counsel or advice. This book and its contents are not intended for the purpose of buying a franchise. This book is a tool that might possibly be helpful in the process of evaluating a franchise business prior to investing in it. Some chapters in the book include sponsored advertising content provided by franchisors to tell their story. No one should invest in a franchise or any business based solely on the information in this book. Investing in a franchise is a serious matter that requires thorough investigation of the franchise opportunity, the franchisor, and related subjects. Franchising is not for everyone. The reader is advised to consult with a licensed professional for legal, financial and other professional services. The reader of this book assumes responsibility for the use of this information. The author and publisher assume no responsibility or liability whatsoever for the use or misuse of the information contained within this book.

Table of Contents

12 Amazing Franchise Opportunities
Includes Sponsored Advertising Content

Amazing Franchise Tools

Foreword

Amazing...*causing great surprise or wonder; astonishing* according to the dictionary. But isn't franchising all about standards, consistency and predictable outcomes?

It certainly is!

Yet, the "amazing" part is how you can participate in a business model where you reap the reward for your efforts *and* you benefit from the collective efforts of the network, including the other franchisees, the vendor partners and the franchise concept owner.

On the planet today, there is no other model that can provide this type of leverage and synergy for anyone seeking the independence of business ownership.

Welcome to **12 Amazing Franchise Opportunities**, a unique collection of interesting, compelling and dynamic concepts offered through the powerful franchise model to average investors. I have spent almost 30 years participating in the franchise sector, mostly as a franchisor, but also as a franchisee, consultant and educator, and there is no better time than now to foray into this entrepreneurial arena.

In this book, Dr. John Hayes masterfully compiles and presents a cadre of concepts destined for greatness, providing readers with a qualified funnel from over 3,000 franchise concepts down to 12 that are worthy of consideration. As you dive into the chapters a vivid rainbow of opportunities emerges, taking your mind on a roller coaster ride of potential as you imagine yourself at the helm of each concept in your hometown.

Ponder how you could embrace, enhance and expand one of these amazing franchises through your personal network, your social influence and your business acumen. Consider the value you could create partnering with a franchisor that provides training, technology, resources and support along your journey. Relish in the knowledge that your efforts would be matched by the others in the franchise network to create a return beyond your capabilities alone. This is the magic of franchising and herein are 12 Amazing Franchises!

Centuries ago, the Kings of old realized the power of the franchise model, granting villagers the "independence and freedom" to be a blacksmith, a farmer or a cobbler, providing needed services to their communities. The King granted them this "franchise" to pursue their passion and their trade, and to reap as much benefit as was possible, so long as they provided a "royalty to the King."

Today, these 12 "Kings" provide you the grant of independence and freedom to reap as much benefit as you can, operating as an independent business owner, so long as you share a small portion with the King to provide support to the kingdom.

It is a simple concept that has created countless millionaires and provided countless families with a lifestyle other families only dream of possessing. Yet, many will stay safely on their couch refusing to take that next important step of discovery which may well lead to the personal satisfaction they desire. Don't let this opportunity pass you by; embrace it and see where it leads.

For over a decade I have taught executives the franchise model through the Certificate in Franchise Management Program at Georgetown University's School of Continuing Studies in Washington, D.C. They come from all across the U.S. and around the world to gain a critical understanding of this most powerful of all business models, hoping to extract even a modicum of its potential to transform their concept into a globally recognized brand.

Yet, none of them will succeed without highly motivated franchisees who provide the local attention to the brand needed to make it personal. The competitive advantage of franchisees is their ability to connect with their community, navigate the pulse of the local economy and field the best team possible on the street. Every brand needs ambassadors to bring their concepts to life in the local community and every franchisor wants to engage with the highest quality individuals to represent their concepts as if it were truly their own.

As you shift through the 12 Amazing Franchises in Dr. Hayes' Second Edition, consider what you bring to the potential relationship with a franchise:

your personal talent, a strong connection to a local marketplace, hard-earned capital that deserves an above-market rate of return and a commitment to contributing to the value of the brand to the good of the overall network.

You should expect from your franchisor partner an equal commitment to continuous monitoring of the marketplace and modifications to the system as needed, the foresight to anticipate challenges and provide you with strong leadership to power through them, and a relentless focus on building brand value, the common denominator in the franchise equation.

The power of franchising has never been as strong as it is now, and it is a testament to the collective efforts of each participant in the network. It is critical that each participant in a franchise be willing to "give up their personal preference for the good of the network," and when that culture of collective effort pervades a brand, everyone associated with the brand benefits, including the customers served.

At the end of the day, the customers will decide the ultimate value of any business and any brand. And when the customer response is strong, the benefits to the network are amazing…higher pricing, stronger margins, exponential resale value. Take advantage of this unique opportunity afforded you by Dr. Hayes to gain a glimpse inside **12 Amazing Franchise Opportunities** and take a journey of discovery that could well lead to the proverbial pot of gold.

Be discerning, ask the difficult questions, and do your homework…franchising is no guarantee of success. But for those that persevere to find the right concept for their ability, the right fit for their market and the right investment for their budget they may well join the ranks of millions that have gone before to a life of independence as a business owner without having to invent the business. And that is truly amazing!

— Dr. Ben Litalien, CFE

Dr. Ben Litalien is a professor in franchising for the University of Maryland University College and at Georgetown University's School of Continuing Studies. He has practiced in franchising for almost three decades, owning and operating franchises in the automotive, foodservice and hospitality sectors. He consults with a wide variety of firms on building franchise concepts including IKEA, ExxonMobil, The UPS Store and RE/MAX. He resides in Stafford County, Virginia with his wife of 32 years. They have three children and four grandsons. He enjoys spending time at their cabin in West Virginia, fly-fishing whenever possible. Reach Dr. Litalien via email ben@franchisewell.com or visit his website at FranchiseWell.com.

Introduction

If you already know about franchising and you think it's an amazing concept, you may want to skip the Introduction and head directly into the chapters to read about the amazing franchise opportunities presented in this book. But if you're curious about why I think franchising is amazing, and you want to know more about what's in this book, please continue reading.

The first time a franchisor explained to me how franchising works, I thought the concept was amazing. After building a successful business, a franchisor offers (of course, for a fee) to teach others how to operate the same business in a different location or market. Amazing...and here's why.

Got an Amazing Idea?

Most people can't come up with a good business idea, let alone know how to build a prototype and successfully open the doors to paying customers. Most people are going to trip up over where to locate the business, or how to negotiate with suppliers, or how to market and advertise the business, or how to charge for products or services, or how to keep customers coming back time after time, or all of that and more.

In other words, most people who start a business are going to fail, and they do. Every year would-be business owners lose billions of dollars in America alone, all because they didn't know what successful franchisors know.

The Secret is in the System

You'll notice that I said "successful franchisors" because not everyone who becomes a franchisor succeeds. But successful franchisors, those who invest the time and the money—especially the money—to build profitable and satisfying businesses also develop a series of systems that they can transfer and teach to other people: franchisees. Everything that successful franchisors know becomes part of a system. And it's the system that franchisees rely on to replicate the franchisor's success.

How does McDonald's eliminate the guesswork about where to open a new unit? That knowledge is part of McDonald's site selection system.

How does a McDonald's franchisee know how many hamburger rolls to purchase on any given day, and how many employees to schedule to operate the business during an eight-hour shift? The answers are part of McDonald's operating system.

In fact, you can't ask a question that McDonald's, the franchisor, can't answer about how to operate a successful McDonald's restaurant. And now, just imagine, McDonald's is willing to share all of its knowledge with you, or any qualified prospect, to become a franchisee anywhere in the world. Tell me that's not amazing!

You Can Minimize the Risk

What's more amazing, and this is what I thought about the first time a franchisor explained franchising to me, is that I do not have to come up with a good business idea, go into debt to develop the idea in the hopes that it would become a profitable and satisfying business, and then fail.

I don't have to take that risk because there are at least 3,000 different franchise opportunities in North America alone. It's easier to find a business concept that I like, and then pay the franchisor to teach me how to operate the business successfully in a new location. Or, I can buy an existing franchise business and bypass the more treacherous start-up years.

I didn't come from a business-minded family, so I knew very little about how to develop and operate a business. And yet, I wanted to own a business because I knew that working for someone else wasn't going to fulfill my life-long expectations. I was never going to make enough money working for someone else, and I'm not a 9-to-5 type of employee.

But until I learned about franchising, I didn't think I could ever own a business. I've since owned several franchises, I've been the CEO of a major franchisor organization, and I've devoted a career to advising franchisors and franchisees, writing about franchising, and teaching people how to take advantage of this amazing concept.

Franchising is an Equalizer

Through the years I've become acquainted with countless people internationally who told me they didn't think they had a chance to own a business because of their circumstances. Some of these people had great ideas for new businesses, but most of them did not have the money to start a business, and many of them did not have a formal education. In fact, several never graduated from high school. No one claimed to know how to build a business.

But once these people discovered franchising, most of their doubts and limitations disappeared over time, and they built profitable and satisfying businesses, and in some cases, financial empires.

It's important to know, as successful franchisors and franchisees will tell you, that while franchising levels the playing field so that most everyone can succeed in business, it doesn't suddenly make everything all right. It makes everything possible, at least in terms of developing a successful business, but it doesn't remove all the risks or limitations, and it surely doesn't do the work for you. Many people are fond of saying that franchising is "turnkey," and unfortunately that leads some people to believe that all they have to do is get the key, turn it, and voila!, success. But it's not that amazing!

Franchising isn't a miraculous solution. I don't know any lazy or uninformed people who have succeeded in franchising. Conversely, of the successful franchisors and franchisees I know, none is a genius. Most are simply hard-working, curious, ambitious people. Some earned college degrees; others did not. Some had family money; most did not. Many struggled before they succeeded, and some failed and started again, but none gave up.

Other than franchising as a common bond, successful franchisors and franchisees also share the ability to be led. Obviously, franchisees need to learn how to be successful in business—that's the purpose of the franchisor's system— but franchisors are not infinitely wise; the best of them recognize that they need to be taught and guided, too, and they invest time and money in their continuing educations. Anyone who isn't willing to be led to greater accomplishments isn't cut out for franchising, as amazing as it may be.

But is Franchising for You?

Even if you agree with me that franchising is amazing, you ultimately have to decide if franchising is for you. You may already have decided that it is and that's why you're reading this book, or you may still be searching for answers even while you're searching for an amazing franchise opportunity. Either way, this book can help you make the decision. Because even though the book is devoted to telling you about 12 amazing franchise opportunities, I've also included additional information that will help you not only decide if franchising is for you, but if it is, what type of franchise is best for you.

Here's What's in the Book

The book includes important information about how to buy a franchise opportunity, sharing step-by-step instructions for making a good buying decision, including many of the questions you should ask. Check out "17 Steps to Successfully Buying a Franchise" and "How to Investigate Before You Invest in a Franchise." If you will need money to buy a franchise, I've covered that for you, too. You'll want to read "Funding Your Franchise Acquisition: Where Do You Get the Money?"

If you're not an American citizen, but you want to use your investment in a franchise or in franchising to move to America under the EB-5 Foreign Investor Program, you'll want to read "Use Franchising to Get Your U.S. Green Card."

Are you a Good Fit for Franchising?

Perhaps the most important chapter—the one you should read first—is "Match Your Personality to the Appropriate Franchise Opportunities." I can't say it often enough: As amazing as it is as a business development methodology, franchising is not for everyone. You can try to force a round peg into a square hole, but you know that's not going to work successfully. All that's going to do is create frustration and possibly a huge financial loss. So why not verify your compatibility with franchising before investing your money? It's easy to do (visit www.howtobuyafranchise.com/disc), it's free, and you'll find out how in this book.

The 12 chapters that describe amazing franchise opportunities were provided by the franchise companies to tell their stories. Prior to each of these chapters I include information about why I believe each franchise opportunity is amazing.

Franchising Caters to Your Desires

Here's another amazing fact about franchising. There's something for (almost) everyone!

- You want to work from home? You can.
- You want to work from a truck? You can.
- You want to work in a store at the mall or a strip center? You can.
- You want to provide a service instead of selling a product? You can.
- You want to own multiple units of the same franchise brand? You can.
- You want to own multiple franchise brands? You can.
- You want to own a territory in which you sell the franchises and then train and support the franchisees while also owning your own unit? You can.
- You want to live the life of an expat building an international franchise empire? You can.

The opportunities are endless. If franchising makes sense for you—and it does not for everyone—then it's a matter of finding the right opportunity. There's a good chance you'll find the right opportunity in this book. In fact, there's a good chance you'll find multiple right opportunities in this book. When you do, your next step is to request information from the franchisors. For now, the only thing left to do is continue reading and find an amazing franchise opportunity that makes sense for you!

Dr. John P. Hayes
January 2018

Is Franchising for You?

One of the most important lessons that I've learned through the years is that many of the people who could be successful franchisees fail as franchisees simply because they bought the wrong franchise.

Granted, some people fail because they are not cut out for franchising, and regardless of which franchise they buy, or how much money they invest, they are destined to fail. I can't say this often enough: Franchising is not for everyone!

It's easy to discover if franchising is for you, so I hope you'll take the time to find out. If it is for you, it's also easy to discover the type of franchise that's best suited for you.

Sadly, many people miss this information and that's why I'm placing this chapter at the front of this book. I not only don't want you to miss it, but I don't think you should pursue any franchise opportunity until you know if you're a good fit for franchising. Why invest the time and the money? Why put yourself at risk?

The last thing you need—the last thing franchising needs—is a business failure. Many franchisee failures, and many of the situations that result in disgruntled franchisor/franchisee relationships (which ultimately tarnish franchising's reputation), could be avoided if people just paid attention to the information in this chapter.

Failed Franchisees Missed this Lesson

This is one of the most important lessons that you, as a prospective franchisee, can learn about franchising. Do yourself the favor that many franchisees before you did not do—learn this lesson and follow it!

Every franchisor should pay attention to this lesson, too, and implement the protective steps that will help their franchisees succeed. But there's another pertinent truth that you should know about franchising: Franchisors are not created equal! Some care more about selling franchises than they care about the success and satisfaction of franchisees.

My Personal Experience with Profiling

My personal story explains why I'm adamant about franchise profiling. The founder of the franchise company, HomeVestors of America, Inc., where I eventually served as president and CEO, died unexpectedly. Ken D'Angelo was a magnificent person, and one of the most conscientious franchisors, and unfortunately, he died at a time when his company was moving from a start-up to a professionally run organization. He had developed a time-tested operating system, the only one of its kind that taught people from all walks of life how to buy and sell real estate for a profit. I was not only an adviser to Ken, but I served on his Board of Directors. I also owned a HomeVestors franchise, which was operated by my partner.

To Ken, investing in real estate was akin to crossing a busy highway—you had to study the situation, calculate the variables, know where to look and what to look for, and ultimately know when to step out and seize the moment. And to Ken, who had no formal education beyond high school, anyone could follow his amazing system and succeed as a real estate investor. And many people did (especially while sub-prime lending existed).

When I succeeded Ken at his request in 2004, HomeVestors had some 250 franchisees buying almost 10,000 houses a year in 30-some states. The company was essentially a marketing machine for real estate investors. Our "We Buy Ugly Houses" billboard campaigns, along with other advertising, generated upwards of 250,000 leads every year for our franchisees!

Every year, HomeVestors organized an annual meeting where Ken and others provided insights and updates about real estate investing, as well as training, networking, and awards. Lots of awards.

Real estate investors come with big egos—most franchisees come with big egos—and a good way to keep them happy and engaged in your business is to publicly reward them for their achievements. Ken was giving his top-performing franchisees Ford F-150 pickup trucks, as well as trophies and cash.

But now here's the odd twist: The top franchisees weren't necessarily getting the best awards.

Identifying Top Franchisees

Who's a top franchisee? That's no different than asking any business owner: Who's your best customer? But most business owners, including franchisors and franchisees, can't answer that question accurately, so it's not surprising that Ken couldn't, either. In any business, the best customer is the one who comes back time after time and pays you (the business owner) the most money without disrupting your business.

When Ken decided to reward franchisees, he looked at several qualifiers, but essentially, he rewarded those who bought the most houses in a year's time. Made sense to me, but for some reason one day after I was appointed president I asked our financial folks to provide me with a list of franchisees ranked by royalty value. In other words, I said, show me the franchisees in ranked order with the one who paid us the most money in royalties at #1 on the list, and the one who paid us the least money in royalties at #250 (or whatever number was last place) on the list.

"Do We Know these Franchisees?"

When I got the list, I said to my leadership team: Who are these people at the top of the list?

They were not the franchisees we had been awarding year after year. Some were, but most were not. In fact, I had never met some of the franchisees, and in the four years that I had worked closely with Ken, he never mentioned them to me, and I don't think he ever visited them in their markets (and we visited many franchisees every year).

Turns out the top franchisees may also be those you rarely hear from…they do not complain, they do not make requests, they do not (necessarily) want to speak at your meetings and conventions, they do not demand that you come and visit them…they just work the system and, well, make money!

The Top Franchisee Report, as I started referring to that list, triggered a gold mine of information and provided tremendous insight for how we should spend our time as a franchisor. For example, our operations folks spent an inordinate amount of time helping many of the lower-rung franchisees who never seemed to be able to work our system.

We thought that if we spent more time (and money) coaching, training, and encouraging these franchisees, they might eventually catch on and perform better…but there was little evidence of that.

The fact was, the best way to help some of those bottom-rung franchisees was to find a buyer for their franchise and let them move on to another occupation. They were simply not fit for our business, and we should not have sold them a franchise.

"What's Different about These Franchisees?"

After I got over my initial surprise about the contents of the list, I asked another question: Why these franchisees?

Now I wanted to know why the top 25 franchisees were the top 25 franchisees. Why them, and not the bottom 25? Obviously the top 25 paid us the most money. But what were they doing that the bottom 25 were not doing? Or, why were the top 25 so much more capable than the bottom 25?

Best of all, I asked: What can we do to make sure we only award future franchises to people who will show up in the top 25, or help expand the top 25 to the top 50?

There were numerous answers to that question, but one of the most pertinent was: Assess their personalities to make sure they're a fit for our business. Actually, Ken had already been doing that, but now it was time to pay more attention to the results.

We had to be sure we were awarding franchises to people who were a good fit for our business.

Obviously, we hadn't done the best job of that in the past, but now we knew how to improve. In doing so, we'd also improve franchisee morale and satisfaction. And it all worked well, until the Great Recession, but that's an entirely different story.

How to Use Your Assessment

You do not need a franchisor to tell you whether or not you're a good fit for franchising (you can find that out on your own and I'll show you how in a moment), but it would be a huge benefit if a franchisor told you whether or not you were a good fit for their business.

Unfortunately, many (maybe most) franchisors can't do that because (a) they don't know or think it's important, (b) they don't know how, (c) they think it would slow down their sales, and/or (d) they've never profiled their franchisees so they don't know who's best-suited for their business. If I were you, before investing in any franchise, I would insist on getting more of this "intelligence" from a franchisor. Some—but not enough—franchisors use personality assessment tools, and I would favor them.

You can quickly get an assessment of your personality by using the DiSC® assessment at www.howtobuyafranchise.com/disc. DiSC measures your behavioral differences or patterns and is at least a preliminary—and free—assessment of your personality and your compatibility with franchising.

The DiSC Personality Profile is not franchise specific, but it provides interesting insights about an individual's strengths characterized in terms of Dominance, Influence, Steadiness, and Compliance.

A Dominant personality, for example, might do well in a business that depends on the franchisee to generate sales; a Compliant personality probably would not succeed in such a business. However, a Compliant personality might do well in a service business that interacts closely with customers, while a Dominant personality might not succeed in such a business.

The Influencer and Steady personalities are likely to excel in businesses that depend on teamwork. Unlike the Dominant and Competent personalities, the I and S personalities like working with other people. However, these personalities require clear and specific operating systems, and strong franchisor support, to succeed.

Many franchisors use DiSC or some form of it, and as a result they can tell you the behaviors that are most successful (and those that are least successful) in their business. If your behaviors differ from those of the most successful franchisees, you're probably not going to become a profitable and satisfied franchisee in that business. Now wouldn't you really like to know that before investing your money? Shouldn't a franchisor want to know that, too?

Before you go any further in your pursuit of franchising, take the time to assess your personality. It's a good protective measure. It takes about ten minutes to complete the DiSC assessment (www.howtobuyafranchise.com/disc).

Give Yourself an Edge

Franchise companies do not need to rely on personality profiling to be amazing, but amazing franchisors are always interested in a franchise candidate's profiling results and how the results relate to their business. So share your results and ask the franchisors if your behavioral patterns will help you succeed in their business.

Some franchisors, as well as franchise brokers, will ask you to complete their preferred, and sometimes proprietary, assessment, and you should be eager to do so.

Using personality assessments and matching the results to appropriate franchise opportunities levels the playing field and ultimately helps you succeed in franchising. Don't go any further until you identify your personality profile!

— Dr. John P. Hayes
West Palm Beach, Florida

12 Amazing

Franchise Opportunities

PREMIER DOGGY DAY CARE & BOARDING

Pet lovers want the very best care for their animals, and Camp Bow Wow® recognized that sentiment in 2000 when the company opened its first doggy day care and boarding facility. Since then, Camp Bow Wow and its franchisees have set the precedent for premium pet care and carved out a new sector in the now $70 billion pet industry.

Every year, millions of dogs excitedly pull their "parents" through the doors of more than 140 Camp Bow Wow camps in over forty states!

So, what's the key to Camp Bow Wow's success?

"Franchise owners combine their love for animals with a proven business model that generated over $100 million in system-wide sales in 2016," explains Renuka Salinger, vice president of franchise development. "We also strive for continued innovation and technology integration to meet the needs of today's convenience-driven customer."

The franchise's corporate headquarters is staffed by award-winning teams dedicated to the continued growth and success of each individual camp location and the overall brand. Because of the low-risk, high-growth franchise opportunity, Entrepreneur has ranked Camp Bow Wow #1 in category in the Franchise 500 list for three consecutive years.

There's a reason why 95 percent of Camp Bow Wow owners renew their agreements and why 28 percent open additional units. To learn more about this fun and fulfilling opportunity, read the full story and then ask for more information.

— Dr. John P. Hayes

Pawsitive Approach to Dog Care Wins Customer, Franchisee Loyalty

If you own a dog, you can surely relate to the common dilemma that so many pet lovers face: what to do with a beloved best friend while vacationing or traveling on business.

Heidi Ganahl, a doting dog owner herself, ran into this very problem years ago. Then a light bulb went off. That old English Proverb – necessity is the mother of invention – sums up Camp Bow Wow's beginnings. Satisfying a widespread need for fun, compassionate, reliable care seemed like a great business idea, so Ganahl opened Camp Bow Wow's first location in Denver, Colorado, in 2000.

Her innovative idea to style Camp Bow Wow, a Premier Doggy Day Care and Overnight Camp®, after a kids' summer camp was met with appreciative wagging tails and thankful humans. Business took off as man's best friend gave a "paws up" for a doggy camp that was much more enjoyable than the typical stifling and cramped kennels. A second location was soon opened, which was quickly followed by the franchising of Camp Bow Wow in 2003. Paws have been making a steady trail to this leading pet franchise ever since.

Nearly two decades later, this rapidly-expanding dog-friendly franchise could just as well "sit and stay" while riding its current success, but resting easy with its tried-and-true formula isn't the Camp Bow Wow way. As an industry innovator, Camp Bow Wow continues to be a game-changer as it leads the doggy daycare pack.

The franchise's success perfectly positioned Camp Bow Wow to attract the attention of some of the biggest players in the pet-care space, resulting in high profile partnerships designed to successfully propel the company well into the future.

In 2014, Camp Bow Wow was acquired by VCA Animal Hospitals, the largest network of veterinary hospitals in North America. VCA was especially attracted to Camp Bow Wow because they consider it a "smile brand" that focuses on the happy side of pet care. This new access to a wealth of knowledge on canine care deepened the doggy daycare's standards nationwide.

Camp Bow Wow offers an opportunity unmatched
in the doggy daycare industry.

In 2017 Mars, Inc., one of the pet-care industry's major players with its Pedigree and Whiskas food brands, sought to purchase VCA because of its strong portfolio of companies including Camp Bow Wow.

Those strong, forward-thinking investments from Mars and VCA coupled with its rock-solid business model allow Camp Bow Wow to offer an opportunity to franchisees that is unmatched in the doggy daycare industry while positioning the company for significant growth and innovation over the next decade.

To support the rapid growth, Camp Bow Wow has attracted top talent to its leadership team and the result has been record system and unit-level performances. In 2016, for example, Camp Bow Wow generated more than $100 million in revenue.*

But that is only the beginning. Under the direction of this dynamic leadership team, Camp Bow Wow is poised to double the size of the company in the next few years by attracting franchise owners who share their passion for making dogs happy.

And for existing franchisees like Louise McKeown of New Jersey, the future seems very bright.

"It is awesome to be part of a total pet-care team and having resources available through Camp Bow Wow corporate and VCA to ensure the Camp experience is top-notch," she says.

The Best Dog's Life

As a pet owner herself, McKeown understands the importance of a trusted, professionally run doggy daycare. That's what sealed the deal for her when she decided to join the Camp Bow Wow family.

"We are not just a business," she says. "We take care of people's children, no different from a child's daycare or sleepaway camp. We provide great customer service, but mostly we are giving our pup parents peace of mind, comfort, and love. They become our family as well."

Dogs always find huggable humans at Camp Bow Wow.

Anyone who owns a dog can surely relate to the common dilemma that so many pet lovers face: what to do with a beloved best friend while vacationing or traveling on business.

At Camp Bow Wow, dogs get plenty of exercise, are never bored or lonely, always find huggable humans, and aren't home alone to mischievously find ways to be destructive. It's all play, all day, and sweet, comfy puppy dreams at night in their own cozy cabin.

And talk about putting the "wow" in Camp Bow Wow! After a long day, all dogs deserve a Campfire Treat™.

McKeown can relate to owners who scramble last-minute to find quality care. After failing to find pet care near her New Jersey home, driving 45 minutes to the closest doggy daycare and shelling out hundreds of dollars for her Labradoodles, Reilly and Darcy, McKeown realized there was a need in her hometown. She observed how the Camp Bow Wow in Bridgewater, nearly an hour away, was a popular spot as happy pet owners brought their fur babies in and out.

"In my neighborhood and at the dog park that I go to, the discussion every spring was, 'What are you going to do with your dog?' There were no good places, other than a traditional kennel. There was no place to take your dog where you felt good about leaving them," McKeown says.

She and her husband solved that problem when they acquired an existing Camp Bow Wow franchise in nearby Lawrenceville, New Jersey. Since then, they have built another location from scratch in northeastern Philadelphia.

McKeown says that cash flow was positive from the start for their first location, even after investing in upgrades. Their second location has been just as successful.

"This summer, the whole world found us," she says. "We're doing great down here."

That's the norm for Camp Bow Wow franchisees.

"Camp Bow Wow's main focus is the dogs' health and happiness," says Gina Paradiso, who owns two franchises in suburban Denver.

She, too, was looking for a place to board her best friend, a chocolate lab puppy.

"With a blink of an eye, I was owning and operating Camp Bow Wow and doing what I was meant to do," she says. "As an owner, I love this vision and follow it daily."

Life-changing Career Choices

Down in the Houston suburb of Katy, Texas, franchise owner José Morillo says he, too, was on the fence about franchises.

Camp Bow Wow changed his mind.

"Although my due diligence studies showed this to be a good business model, there is always that lingering thought in the back of your head that says, 'Am I making the right choice?'

After visiting a couple of franchise locations and then corporate headquarters in Westminster, Colorado, "that's when I knew what I wanted to be when I grew up," he says. "I went to check it out and I was blown away by the concept. Boy, am I glad I did not listen to that voice. My business is thriving and the future looks bright, indeed."

Morillo now says his career change from hospital CEO to Camp Bow Wow franchisee was the best decision of his life. Morillo no longer works a minimum 60 hours a week while living in a nearby apartment and commuting 90 minutes home on weekends. He hasn't turned back since scouting franchise possibilities.

"In hindsight, it was the craziest thing I've ever done but the best decision I've ever made," he says.

Reaching Out to Corporate America

Morillo has won over a large clientele from nearby buildings. Camp Bow Wow's 401K-9® Employee Benefits Program – a nationwide partnership with corporations (including Academy, Nationwide Insurance and GEICO) and their employees – has helped solidify that market. Benefits include a 10 percent discount on daycare, overnight boarding, and in-home pet-care services. There's also a 5 percent discount on retail sales and special promotions. That's a tremendous savings for loyal customers who frequently entrust their fur babies to Camp Bow Wow.

"Fortune Magazine in a recent article called it the 'humanization of pets.' Humans are treating their dogs as if they were a fellow human," Morillo says. "The pets have become their family. Everything about that is good for the business."

His webcams have been so popular. Clients are also "blown away" by Camp Bow Wow's smartphone app that allows them to keep track of their dogs in the play yard. As a result, Morillo's Texas location, which celebrated two years of business in September 2017, thrives.

"We've ramped up fast. No complaints from me. It's been a great ride so far," he says.

Time for a Vacation

Best of all, as Morillo's daughter-in-law has taken over management duties, he has found life balance, including vacation time. And you can guarantee that he leaves his three Chihuahuas at Camp Bow Wow. Being able to board Pepe, Taco and Trini was part of the decision-making when Morillo and his wife chose a Camp Bow Wow franchise.

For franchisees like Morillo, McKeown and Paradiso, there's definitely peace of mind in knowing that every aspect of running a doggy daycare has already been fine-tuned by the corporate team back in Colorado.

Camp Bow Wow has left nothing to chance. Beyond the day-to-day operations, safety for four-legged guests is at the forefront. Camp Counselors are first aid and CPR trained for pets, just in case. They even have extensive training in dog behavior.

Dogs must be current on vaccinations and be spayed or neutered. Each pet is required to be "interviewed" to make sure they have the right temperament for socializing with others.

"It's a beautiful concept," Morillo notes. "You're not reinventing the wheel. You've got to learn it for the first time, but it's not being done for the first time."

Success by the Numbers

Back on the East Coast, McKeown and her husband, who have both worked on Wall Street, ran the numbers and immediately realized that Camp Bow Wow was the investment they were looking for.

By 2017, the pet industry was projected to reap more than $69 billion from caring pet parents. That's a whopping 40 percent increase from $41.2 billion in 2007, according to the American Pet Product Association (APPA). With about 65 percent of U.S. households owning pets, that's a huge market.

McKeown has noticed a trend: Double-income Millennials are delaying having kids but spare no expense on their dogs.

Empty nesters like the McKeowns often have freed-up cash when their kids are grown that they can spend on their fur babies.

"My daughter thinks I love the dogs more than her," she says.

For Millennials, retirees, and everyone in-between, Camp Bow Wow offers everything busy pet owners need. And that's why Camp Bow Wow works, says Camp Bow Wow President Christina Russell.

Camp Bow Wow is perfectly positioned for dramatic nationwide growth.

"It resonates with the changing way people take care of their dogs," she says. "Pet parents love that Camp Bow Wow lets dogs play all day instead of being locked up."

And the "parents" love the personal touch they receive, as well.

For example, Camp Bow Wow offers added services (creating multiple revenue streams for franchisees) that include dog training, baths, and full-service dog grooming.

"You don't want to pick up a dirty kid at the end of Camp," Russell says with a laugh.

McKeown, like most franchisees, makes a point to be on location as much as possible. Having face time with her customers gives her a chance to thank them for their business.

"It's really gratifying. I know most of my clients," she says. "They love us. We're a vital part of their lives because we're taking care of something that is an equivalent of their child, and they're grateful."

Camp Bow Wow is continually recognized as a leader both locally and nationally.

Award-winning Pet Service

Happy franchisees' success stories speak for themselves, and Camp Bow Wow has the kudos to prove it. They recently garnered the 2017 Silver Stevie Award Winner for National Sales Team of the Year; 2017 Gold Stevie Award

Winner for Marketing Department of the Year; 2016 Gold Stevie Winner for Best Website; 2017 and 2016 Entrepreneur Magazine's Franchise 500 – Ranked #1 in Category; 2017 Entrepreneur Magazine's Franchise 500 – Best of the Best; and has been in Entrepreneur Magazine's Franchise 500 for 10 years running.

These are just the latest in a long line of recognition the chain has received over the years.

The average Camp Bow Wow franchise makes nearly $785,000 in revenue, according to the Financial Performance Representation in Camp Bow Wow's 2017 Franchise Disclosure Document. Top franchisees generate more than $1 million.**

As of 2017, there were 144 locations in 43 states and one location in Canada, with many more on the way, according to Renuka Salinger, vice president of franchise development at Camp Bow Wow. By the end of 2020, Camp Bow Wow hopes to have 300 franchises open with plans to grow worldwide.

And much of that growth is coming from existing franchisees as well as newcomers. In 2011, multi-unit ownership was three percent of franchises. That percentage now stands at 28 percent!

Multi-unit Ownership

"It's huge sign of satisfaction in a franchise community when people want to invest in second and third units and go the multi-unit route. Nothing makes me happier," says Russell. "It means we are doing the right things as a team by showing the care and support we value so much, and creating something that's really fun and life-changing for them."

Russell says she can really wrap her brain around the Camp Bow Wow motto: Happy, Healthy Pets; Happy, Healthy People!

"The word 'happy' reflects our joy about what we do, and that's rare when you think about big companies like this. I love that we get to focus on that happiness and joy," she says.

A Focus on Innovation

Innovation is another reason that franchisees – like pet owners -- continue to flock to Camp Bow Wow from across the U.S.

Camp Bow Wow has had its own state-of-the-art CRM system for over half a decade and is continually updating and innovating its technology. And the acquisitions by VCA and Mars have provided the company with the resources to significantly enhance its capabilities.

As a result of the VCA acquisition, for example, Camp Bow Wow was able to introduce its own app for clients that delivers real-time updates, photos and other communications to pet owners.

"Pet care is going through an 'uberization,'" says Russell. "We want to make the entire process convenient and simple for pet owners and our advanced technology allows us to do that."

Not only does this innovation attract customers, but it has also proven an important differentiator for franchisees.

"In many ways, we are really a technology company," says Russell. "No one else in the industry is doing what we are doing and our advanced level of sophistication is what is attracting more and more franchisees."

Puppy Love and Business Savvy

While hanging out with dogs sounds like heaven for anyone who loves dogs, running a franchise goes way beyond. "Must Love Dogs" is only the tip of the iceberg.

Camp Bow Wow is very selective in choosing franchisees, says Salinger, who started working at Camp Bow Wow as a Camp Counselor right after college.

From more than 3,000 leads Camp Bow Wow receives every year, only 20 to 40 percent are truly qualified. Camp Bow Wow knows its pet parents expect nothing but the best for their four-legged children. Great care is taken in selecting potential franchisees who not only love pets but are business smart and motivated.

"At the end of the day, I love dogs, but trust me, it's also a serious business," McKeown says. "Today I went to BJ's [Wholesale Club] to get 28 boxes of dog treats, solved employee issues and scheduled an HVAC guy to change my filters. It's not just dogs."

Camp Bow Wow's track record with franchisees is impressive. Russell notes that, "95 percent of our 10-year agreements turn into 20-year agreements. It's almost like a marriage."

Ongoing Support

Paradiso knew right away that Camp Bow Wow had her back because they were "warm and inviting from the start. They are always available for questions, concerns, and help. They made the experience feel very personal."

When McKeown was building her Philadelphia, Pennsylvania, location from the ground up, no detail was too small that the corporate team at Camp Bow Wow hadn't already thought of, including the best building layout for workflow and even the plumbing.

When something went terribly wrong, McKeown knew that help was only a phone call away. A client had dropped off an elderly dog despite warnings from the vet that their pet may not make it until they came back from vacation. When the pet passed away, McKeown reached out to an area director.

"That ability to have someone to call was amazing. I have his cell phone number. It was a Saturday and I got ahold of him."

Franchisees also have each other as a sounding board, to exchange ideas, and for moral support. For McKeown, that is huge.

"The franchise community is great."

More Information

Camp Bow Wow's continued success means more opportunities for business-minded pet lovers. If a Camp Bow Wow franchise piques your interest, contact Renuka Salinger, vice president of franchise development, at 720-259-2293, or visit their website: www.campbowwowfranchise.com.

Figure represents the aggregate Gross Revenue for all locations that were open and operating in 2016, including those owned by the Franchisor or its predecessor.

**Figures represent averages for the 118 revenue-reporting franchises open and operating for more than 12 months during the 12-month period ending on December 31, 2016. Of all 118 franchises, 52 exceeded the average of \$784,781. Of the 30 Franchises representing the top 25%, 10 (33%) exceeded the average of \$1,149,950. Of the 30 Franchises representing the bottom 25%, 19 (63%) exceeded the average of \$465,967. The financial performance representation contained in Item 19 of our 2017 Franchise Disclosure Document also includes: (1) selected expenses for expense-reporting franchises; and (2) system-wide gross revenue.

Xpresso*delight*

TASTE *THE* DIFFERENCE

When it comes to developing franchise concepts, America leads the world, but every so often a concept pops up in another country and then travels to the U.S. Thus is the case with Xpresso Delight, developed by Australians and now expanding into America.

People everywhere love good coffee, and while America has plenty of coffee shops and coffee brewing methodologies, there's a growing demand for better coffee, especially in offices. Think about the lapse in office productivity when employees feel the urge to run out for a good cup of coffee. What's it take? Ten to thirty minutes, two or more times a day?

Xpresso Delight gives business owners a way to provide high-quality coffee while keeping employees productively engaged at the office. The company places (and does not sell) a European-engineered coffee machine in offices, and employees can serve themselves the coffee of their choice as often as they like. The business pays per cup of coffee served, and thus employers enjoy higher employee output.

Xpresso Delight franchisees are responsible for placing machines in offices and maintaining the coffee makers on a weekly basis. The machine does everything else, including tracking how many cups of coffee are served. All billing is handled by the franchisor.

For people seeking a home-based franchise opportunity with a low upfront investment, Xpresso Delight may be the answer. This opportunity allows franchisees to decide if they'll work full- or part-time. On average, a franchisee spends thirty to forty-five minutes maintaining each machine weekly, and the number of hours worked in a week depends on the number of machines placed.

Interested? The next chapter offers an in-depth look at Xpresso Delight. When you're finished reading, just ask for more information.

— Dr. John P. Hayes

Xpresso Delight Offers a "Latte"
More Than Plain Office Coffee

When you think of gourmet coffee, the office break room typically doesn't spring to mind as the place to grab the ultimate java fix. You're more apt to find a K-Cup brewer or coffee pot sitting on the shelf, accompanied by powdered or pre-packaged creamer that has been around for who knows how long. That's not exactly fresh or inviting.

A gourmet coffee fix typically requires a trip to the local coffee shop down the street. But who has time in their day to keep running out of the office for fresh gourmet coffee and espresso drinks – and, let's be honest, who has the budget?

The solution is Xpresso Delight, a franchise opportunity just arriving in the United States from Australia, where the brand has changed the way employees experience coffee in the office.

"In Australia today, as a nation we consume around 1.6 billion espresso coffees a year – incredible numbers for a population of only 25 million," says co-founder Paul Crabtree. "But the number is even more incredible when you consider that over 70 percent of all espresso coffees are consumed by workers going to work or having those coffees in the morning while at work."

By capitalizing on the growing popularity of gourmet coffee in the workplace, Xpresso Delight has grown to almost 200 franchisees in Australia and New Zealand and has reaped an incredibly strong roster of awards and accolades in Australia, including: BRW Top Fastest Growing Franchise for 5 years in a row (2008-2012); Number 1 Franchise System in the "lifestyle" category from topfranchise.com.au; named among Top 10 Franchise Awards on Channel 9's A Current Affair.

Now they have their sights set on America, and Crabtree sees the current U.S. coffee market where the Australian market was about 10 years ago.

Time for a Change in Work/Life Balance

In the early 2000s, Crabtree was working 80-90 hours a week in his corporate, business-to-business-focused company in Australia. He had a young family, and the work/life balance was deeply lacking. He knew he wanted three things:

- A 20- to 30-hour workweek, giving him more time with his family;
- No hiring or managing employees;
- A way to generate a decent income in a short amount of time.

This seemed like the perfect business path, but the reality was much different with long hours, little passion for the job he was doing, and even less time for the family.

So Crabtree decided it was time to do something about his situation. He started to investigate snack vending machine businesses because they checked all of his business requirements. The simplicity of a vending business appealed to him – because of the semi-passive income nature.

It turns out that the market was already saturated with vending companies, and many businesses already had contacts and vendors they were using. He couldn't get his foot in the crowded door.

As he went back to the drawing board, Crabtree came across a concept utilizing café-style espresso coffee machines that ground coffee on demand from fresh whole beans and incorporated fresh milk on a per-cup basis, recreating the cafe experience so prevalent in Australian homes and businesses. Crabtree knew that the number of savvy, educated coffee drinkers was booming, so he bought 10 machines on the spot. The timing turned out to be perfect.

In 2003, Crabtree and co-founder Stephen Spitz purchased additional machines and created Xpresso Delight. They targeted a largely untapped market opportunity that provided an easy, affordable espresso coffee solution to the modern workplace.

After enjoying incredible success in Australia,
Xpresso Delight expects even greater results in the U.S.

Crabtree and Spitz set up the espresso machines in offices of their business contacts, formulated a unique proprietary coffee blend, and created a service system that could be duplicated easily by anyone. Within two weeks, the business had earned a quick $2,000. Former contacts, who had become accustomed to seeing Crabtree in suit and tie, were instantly interested in how they could become a part of this new opportunity. To meet that demand, the Xpresso Delight franchise opportunity was launched.

"Transplanting the Café Experience into the Workplace"

The concept behind Xpresso Delight is actually incredibly simple – and that's the real beauty of it. Crabtree created a strong business model that allows franchisees to leverage their time to the fullest while giving corporate office workers the ultimate café experience.

The Xpresso Delight mission is to deliver an amazing café experience through.

- A fully automated coffee machine
- A unique proprietary coffee blend
- Exceptional customer service

"Xpresso Delight is a simple business concept that virtually anyone can operate," says Crabtree. "Specifically, we transplant the café experience into your workplace. We are in partnership with our franchisees and encourage great work ethic, excellent customer service, and the importance of work/life balance. We want our franchisees to enjoy their business and not be run by it."

Franchisees own the fully automated gourmet espresso coffee systems, manufactured to exacting standards in Switzerland and equipped with state-of-the-art technology. A patented auto-cappuccino mechanism produces a hot, creamy froth so thick that cinnamon and hot cocoa floats on top of the drink made with fresh milk.

So how do franchisees make a profit? The coffee systems are given away FREE to businesses, but franchisees service the coffee systems weekly, providing all the consumables except for fresh milk. They then charge their clients a small per-cup rate. Xpresso Delight even supplies its own proprietary blend of coffee, which is roasted fresh every week and shipped directly to the client.

There are no upfront costs or contracts for the businesses using Xpresso Delight, and because the franchisees own the coffee system, clients receive a lifetime warranty.

Getting to the "Beans" of the Business

One key element of Xpresso Delight's franchise operations is a central billing structure that eliminates the hassle of invoicing and collecting for the franchisee. Clients receive one invoice a month, which is generated from the electronic "per cup counter" on their espresso machine. This is recorded when the franchisee services the machine each week. Xpresso Delight invoices the franchisee's client and pays the franchisee after accounts are settled.

For the franchisee, it has proven to be a simple process that does not require a major time commitment. Franchisees typically spend an average of one hour per coffee machine per client per week. They can run the business by themselves if they don't want to manage employees and payroll.

"The reality is that the machine does the majority of the work and franchisees are able to enjoy a flexible lifestyle while also running their own business," says Crabtree.

The goal of each Xpresso Delight franchisee is to provide a personalized, "5 Star Concierge Coffee Service."

Franchisees take care of everything, from servicing the machines to maintaining customer relationships. In those rare cases when a machine stops working properly, Xpresso Delight has a 4-hour service guarantee and will repair the machine onsite or have the machine replaced within 24 hours. Repairs are completed at NO COST to the client.

Xpresso Delight also is focused on being environmentally friendly in its business practices, using 'bean to cup' machines, meaning plastic capsules or paper filters are not needed to produce a perfectly brewed cup of coffee. This sustainability cuts down operating costs and leaves a very small waste footprint, which is increasingly important in businesses across the globe.

An Amazing 'Jolt' for U.S. Coffee Service

After making their mark on the Australian coffee market, Crabtree and Xpresso Delight's COO Nigell Lee have now focused their attention on the U.S. After studying the U.S. coffee market for several years, they believe the U.S. market is where the Australian market was when Xpresso Delight was born.

"About 70 to 80 percent of offices in Australia have an espresso coffee machine. In the U.S., less than five percent of offices have one," says Lee, who is leading the franchising charge in the U.S.

Lee sees a trend among employees, especially younger ones, to leave the office to purchase an expensive cup of coffee from down the street rather than settle for the traditional, tasteless cup of office coffee. To satisfy this demand, companies increasingly are looking for ways to easily and affordably provide "barista-quality" coffee in their place of work.

According to Lee, a study of the American market found that in about 90 to 95 percent of the territories studied, there was no bean-to-cup facility. They also determined that there are currently two OCS (office coffee service) market segments that offer two completely different offerings and experiences:

Segment 1: Existing pre-ground coffee pot and capsules market (Keurig, Flavia, etc).

Segment 2: A new and evolving fresh bean/fresh milk café-quality coffee experience market.

Segment 1 is around 99 percent and oversaturated, while Segment 2 has approximately 2 to 3 percent market penetration and is nearly 98 percent underserviced. Xpresso Delight is positioned to take on Segment 2, already proving that success in Australia.

"We see an untapped potential of 800,000 to 850,000 qualified businesses that could become Xpresso Delight customers in the U.S.," says Lee. A "qualified" business consists of 20 or more employees. "Potential Xpresso Delight qualified businesses are becoming aware of this new espresso coffee service but are not aware of what the solution is or how to obtain it. We know how to get this new and evolving market."

Crabtree and Lee have yet to see any major competitors in the U.S. that deliver a similar product: a combination of freshly roasted and ground beans and fresh milk to create gourmet coffee drinks in-office on a pay-per-cup model.

"It's a concept that has been flying under the radar, and it is primed and ready for the U.S. corporate business office," says Lee.

Crabtree and Lee realize that the challenge for any non-U.S. brand is credibility, and they are eager to establish the brand. They signed their first two franchise agreements in New York and Connecticut in late 2017. The goal is to sell to Area Developers from the top 60 MSA territories as well as single unit franchisees to help support brand growth.

The 'Perks' of an Xpresso Delight Franchise

An Xpresso Delight franchise offers its franchisees an amazing opportunity to create their own business and generate high leverage on their own time. Yet at the same time, franchisees are able to tap into the support of experienced professionals who have done it all before.

The corporate support staff helps franchisees develop a business plan that will bring goals into focus and then train them how to operate and service the machines.

Additionally, franchisees receive assistance in developing the necessary business, sales, and marketing skills to manage and grow the business.

Once franchisees are operational, Xpresso Delight has local area developers for face-to-face support and is always available by phone, email, or text.

This level of support has created raving fans among franchisees in Australia, like Gus Battaliou in Eatons Hill.

"It had to be a dynamic franchise, one that had good growth potential, which provided flexible working hours and that had a product that I would be proud to sell," Battaliou says. "Xpresso Delight fulfilled what I was looking for. The excellent backup and systems has made the transition to Xpresso Delight an absolute pleasure. Some of my customers cannot start the day properly until they have had their 'coffee fix,' and that satisfaction lingers knowing that you have provided them with an excellent start to their day."

Future Business is 'Brewing' for Xpresso Delight

Now Crabtree and Lee are ready and eager to further forge into the U.S. market with Xpresso Delight. The businesses that have already begun to utilize the service are providing rave reviews, such as this one from a customer in Australia:

"Our team has had the pleasure of using an Xpresso Delight machine for over a year, and we cannot recommend a better system for quick and delicious in-office specialty coffees. The machine is simple to use and delivers popular drinks such as cappuccinos, espressos, lattes, macchiatos, and more."

New York franchisee Matthew Dwyer was looking for a fitting franchise opportunity that was scalable and would work in tandem with his existing full-time job. Since launching his Xpresso Delight franchise in the New York market, he has already experienced better-than-expected results in just one month. Dwyer is looking forward to seeing how big he can scale the business.

"I've been looking for the right franchise opportunities for years. Laundromats, restaurants, technology services, signage, all required too much time and capital to get started. Plus, I didn't see a big differentiator that would enable me to scale up quickly. Xpresso Delight met all my requirements, including low startup costs, limited time commitments, as I already have a full-time job, and fantastic startup support from my Area Developer. There's no one (yet) in the U.S. market that I've come across positioning office coffee systems on a consumption model. The whole system basically sells itself and my customers love the simplicity of the service. My goal was to place two machines a month, but I was able to place six machines in just my first month! I'm really excited to see how big I can scale the business!"

Lee expects feedback like this to become commonplace once the Xpresso Delight concept has spread across the U.S. He and Crabtree hope that companies will appreciate Xpresso Delight's in-house offerings, which will eliminate any need for employees to leave the office for gourmet coffee, compromising work time. For franchisees, finding a business opportunity that allows a healthy work/life balance while establishing income on their own terms definitely sweetens the deal.

More Information

For more information on the "perks" of owning an Xpresso Delight in the U.S., visit www.xdcoffee.com or contact Nigell Lee, COO, at 866-XPRESSO (977.3776) or nigell.lee@xpressodelight.com.

Commercial Cleaning Services

V alues in business make a difference not only to customers but franchisees, too, and Office Pride's core values provide a distinguishing characteristic for this franchise opportunity.

Office Pride Core Values:

- Integrity
- Professionalism
- Exceeding Expectations

In addition, Office Pride was founded on and operates on Biblical principles. This twenty-five-year-old franchise system is easy to learn, operate and grow, and the franchisor's greatest desire is for every franchisee to succeed happily!

Office Pride is committed to educating prospective franchisees, helping them learn as much as possible about franchising – and the Office Pride opportunity – before investing money. That's part of the company's commitment to their core values.

This franchise company has participated in Franchise Business Review's annual franchisee satisfaction survey for eleven years and has consistently scored ahead of most franchise opportunities. In the 2017 survey, for example, Office Pride was ranked #7 for large franchise networks (120-299 units), #25 in the "Best of the Best Overall Top 50," and . . . drum roll . . . #1 among commercial cleaning franchises in the Cleaning and Maintenance category. That's amazing!

Looking for a franchise opportunity that provides recurring income, a family focus, and cherished values? Keep reading: You've found it with Office Pride.

— Dr. John P. Hayes

Core Values Are a Clean Sweep for
Devoted "Family" of Franchisees

Core Beliefs and Values are the guiding principles for the Office Pride devoted 'family' of franchisees. Those Office Pride Beliefs and Values, based on Biblical principles, are what continue to attract franchisees to Office Pride and have them saying it was the best business and career decision they've ever made.

Office Pride has laid the foundation for scalable and sustainable growth by building a franchise business system and support team that is focused on franchisee unit performance, operational efficiency and bottom-line growth.

When it comes to franchisee and customer service satisfaction, Office Pride gets an A+ for its focus on building mutually beneficial relationships based on honesty, integrity and a hard work ethic. As for Office Pride franchisees, it's all about the culture and mutual support, friendship, family and faith.

Making a Connection

For Julie and Kevin McAdoo from Florida, it was an easy transition from their roles in the U.S. Air Force as a pilot and navigator, respectively.

"Coming from careers that were based on values, that was the thing that made Office Pride stand out and appeal to us," says Julie, a Tampa franchisee.

Jason Courtney, who started out cleaning for Office Pride and moved up through the ranks, found his niche from the moment he left the restaurant business behind and signed on with the commercial cleaning business. He has been the proud owner of a franchise in Pensacola, Florida, since 2015.

"The fact that it's a Christian-based organization was a big influencer. Their core values align with my core values," he says.

Scott and Carmen Ramsey can relate. They were slowly building their own cleaning business when a friend recommended Office Pride.

"The core values with Office Pride really hit home with us," Scott says.

The Ramseys bought an existing franchise in Terre Haute, Indiana, and they say the move has had a positive impact on their lives ever since.

"Sometimes you just know it's going to be a good fit. We liked it being a faith-based business," says Carmen, who left an administrative job to start their first cleaning business.

"What really pushed us to break out and pursue it was that we wanted to be in control. It was a means of bettering our lives," she says. "When Office Pride presented itself as a faith-based business, we were really impressed."

Once their new venture at Office Pride was on solid footing, Scott was able to jump onboard after taking a buyout from a middle-management position at a local college.

Carmen says that she and Scott both struggled to find fulfillment and a life balance as they raised their blended family with four "his and her" children. As they leaned on faith to figure it out, they know that Office Pride coming along when it did was a godsend.

Scott and Carmen Ramsey are fulfilling the dream of spending more time with their kids as business owners thanks to Office Pride.

Founded on Faith

Office Pride, founded by Todd Hopkins in 1992 in Indiana, may not be the biggest commercial cleaning business, but Hopkins takes pride in the philosophy that Office Pride is the best franchise system and the best place for franchisees to realize their dreams. Scott and Carmen can't say enough about how Office Pride stays true to its word.

Hard work with honesty and integrity – from corporate all the way to cleanup crew – is what keeps clients coming back. Office Pride boasts a near 90 percent retention rate of its clientele.

Compare that to about 60 percent in the commercial cleaning industry as a whole.

"We're able to retain our customers with processes that corporate teaches us through great customer service and building relationships," says Jason, who is proud of his Pensacola franchise's 92 percent retention rate. "Many competitors would rather spend money on getting new customers than keep the ones they have. They focus on getting the new in and don't focus on serving the old, but we do both.

That's where we stand out."

A commitment to its franchisees has earned Office Pride national recognition.

Kudos for Cleaning

Franchisees have shown their continued satisfaction with Office Pride's approach to cleaning and business acumen through their glowing satisfaction scores, including Franchise Business Review's (FBR) Annual Franchise Satisfaction Survey, which recently placed Office Pride in the FBR Hall of Fame. That means Office Pride has consistently placed in the Top 200 franchises for more than 10 years in a row.

Beyond its own franchisees' positive testimonials, Office Pride has racked up a tidy sum of awards within the cleaning industry. Year after year, the company has consistently ranked in the FBR's Top 100 Veterans & Franchising. Office Pride landed at #17 on the Military Times' "Best for Vets" franchise list. The company also has garnered Building Services Contractors Association International (BSCAI) Safety Awards, as well as many Consumer Choice Awards.

Faith, Family, Friends

Perhaps the most fulfilling part of being a franchise partner in the Office Pride network is how Founder Todd Hopkins not only helps his franchisees attain their personal best but how he also treats them like one big family.

As Carmen and Scott Ramsey of Indiana searched for a clear vision of what their future could hold, Scott knew he had found the right fit when he had one of his first one-on-one talks with Hopkins.

"He didn't say, 'How can we teach you more about business?' He said, 'How can we help you fulfill your dream?' That was really eye opening for us. Here was someone who was being concerned and caring about us and our personal goals and trying to help us reach that," Scott says.

Later on, Scott texted Todd, who is a voracious reader, asking for a good book recommendation for an upcoming vacation. As usual, Todd's advice was inspired: The Power of Full Engagement, which Scott says, discusses work-life balance.

"The whole premise is that we have rhythms that we work in, and if you push that to the limit, you have little to no energy and burn yourself out. Make sure you take those breaks and you refresh yourself. If it kills you before you get there, it's kind of a moot point. It's already changing my whole thought process."

Office Pride's training certification program helps franchisees grow both as a business owner and as a person.

Jason, too, has benefited from the Office Pride founder's approach to life and work. With the right managers in place and someone handling sales, Jason works a regular 40-hour workweek. And, as Office Pride sees the big picture as more than day-to-day operations, Jason has taken advantage of opportunities he never dreamed of. Office Pride's training certification program has helped Jason grow as both a franchisee and as a person.

Jason isn't the only one who benefits from that training. New franchisees who request help are the lucky recipients, as well, as they spend invaluable time under a seasoned franchisees' guidance. Experienced folks like Jason travel to the new franchise to share their sales and operations expertise. He recently helped out new franchisees in Overland Park, Kansas, a Kansas City suburb.

"It's been really rewarding being able to work with the groups I've worked with. I didn't expect that when I became an owner," Jason says. "I expected to just focus on my business, but it's been such a family. I'm excited to help new folks."

Those sorts of bonds are an amazing win-win for both new and established franchisees. While new owners learn the ropes, franchisees like Jason are re-energized when he helps others.

"It re-inspired me to come back and really take charge. It motivated me. I wasn't really expecting that when I started my own business, but it's been a real blessing," he says. "It's been a real help for me as well to reignite that flame. Sometimes you get a little tired, but you have to remember what it was like at the beginning."

Julie McAdoo in Tampa has seen firsthand how Office Pride's culture has pushed her to grow in her personal life and her work life, as well as having the opportunity to watch her own employees transform.

"I feel like it has really expanded my worldview tremendously," she says. "I have learned so much about people and business. The most rewarding part is definitely developing my employees. I enjoy watching them grow as professionals and leaders."

Stories of triumph from franchisees like the McAdoos, Ramseys and Courtney are not unusual. Office Pride's proven success is evident as the franchise enjoys a steady growth with more than 135 Office Pride franchises across the U.S. in a $78 billion, recession-resistant commercial cleaning industry.

Down to the Nitty Gritty

Beyond providing professional and personal growth to its franchisees and employees, Office Pride takes immense satisfaction in its approach to leaving every office sparkling clean. Leaving the cleaning to the professionals – with honesty, integrity and commitment every time – is standard practice that customers can consistently count on. And franchisees know how to deliver, thanks to corporate-backed education.

"I love the professional development aspect of being a part of Office Pride," says Julie McAdoo. "I feel like it is a learning organization bent on constant improvement and ever-higher levels of service to its franchisees."

Retaining valued customers is the order of the day as great care is taken in not only the cleaning processes and products used but also in the very best training.

"The training is some of the best in the businesses," says Jason. "They continue to support you with coaching, through a monthly call to keep everybody pumped up and up to date on best practices."

That in-depth training enables franchisees to dive into each project with confidence in Office Pride's tried-and-true process.

For franchisees like the McAdoos, taking that knowledge to employees is key in sustaining customer service.

"The unexpected part is how complicated cleaning can actually be. Everyone assumes that cleaning is simple and straightforward. In reality, there is a lot of ambiguity, and you need cleaners who are professionals and have good judgment," she says.

Clean as a Whistle

Beyond Office Pride's unique approach to business (as they win both franchisee and customer loyalty through their core values), the commercial cleaning franchise also has an exclusive cleaning system and specialized cleaning products that have been researched and tested before ever being implemented.

Office Pride franchisees use Green Seal™ certified commercial cleaning products and the latest equipment, including high filtration vacuums and microfiber mops, for the absolute best clean. Their unique Color-Coded Cleaning System with color-coded cloths used for specific work areas helps keep work environs free of cross-contamination.

Office Pride's skilled professionals offer their clients a Custom Cleaning Specification (CCS), which guarantees meticulous, customized service every time.

Fellow Franchisees, as well as friends, spending time together at the Indy 500 as guests with the founder and President of Office Pride.

Buckets of Goodwill

As with any business, and in life, issues do come up. When any sort of small or not-so-small crisis arrives, these franchisees know that corporate support is only a phone call away. Just like family.

Scott Ramsey says he watched in awe as Office Pride corporate swung into action when a fellow franchisee suffered a heart attack and his wife needed assistance dealing with the day-to-day operations of their business. Office Pride stepped up, no questions asked, so that she could stay right by her husband's side as he recovered.

"The corporate office stepped right in and sent other couples in to cover and help them maintain so they could get through that time without skipping a beat. They went way above and beyond," he says. "When a situation like that happens, you can lose your business just that quick."

But Office Pride isn't about to let their franchisees fail on their watch if they can help it. As Jason Courtney found out, Office Pride truly was there to help when he needed them the most. Floor work for one of his best customers wasn't going well. Jason didn't have the manpower or the equipment to finish the project to meet his own high expectations on time. Instead of panicking, he called Office Pride corporate.

"They sent the director of operations and a van full of equipment. He was there with us for the four-day weekend getting it corrected to make sure the customer was happy before he went back to Tampa," says Jason. He was not only extremely relieved but also thankful that Office Pride helped him handle the situation "in an extremely professional manner."

Time to Admire their Success

With all that hard work, there is time for reflection and camaraderie. Each year, franchisees are invited to an annual retreat where liked-minded owners can swap stories, lend support and ideas, and just relax.

"The best thing about Office Pride is the culture. We love our fellow franchisees and truly benefit from the openness, sharing, and willingness to help each other grow our businesses together," says Julie McAdoo. "It's a wonderful and enriching community, and I am so looking forward to our annual retreat where we get to see owners from around the country, share stories, and share best practices and lessons learned."

The Ramseys didn't always make the retreats initially, but they now make a point to get there each year for some hard-earned back patting and team building opportunities from Office Pride corporate.

"They work hard at helping us celebrate our individual success and celebrating Office Pride success as a whole," says Scott.

Jason, who says he often finds himself listening to music while he works, can't say enough about the mini concerts that Office Pride provides at their Florida retreats. For 2017, contemporary Christian singer and songwriter Phil Wickham performed. That's just one of the nice perks of the corporate getaway.

"It's just a great time to connect with other franchisees, reminding yourself that you're not the only one going through what you're going through that particular day. We're all out there in this together. It really gets us all pumped back up," says Jason.

Mopping up Rewards

That passion for Office Pride is cause for celebration. Jason and his fellow franchisees gather each year to look back and look ahead...together.

And while the kudos and friendships are a great part of their gathering, Julie says it's also a great opportunity to learn new things to take back to their business.

"Todd Hopkins brings in great speakers every year to the retreat. I always feel like their message was made just for me," she says.

Scott and Carmen's franchise has exceeded sales to be a part of Office Pride's Half Million Dollar Club for the past two years.

Last year, Jason's Pensacola franchise was inducted into the Million Dollar Club, as well as being recognized for their community service work with Gulf Coast Kid's House, a nonprofit children's advocacy center for abused and neglected children. Office Pride encourages giving back to the community by offering free cleaning services and manpower. His goal is being awarded with the Two Million Dollar Club this year.

And those Office Pride friendships spill out into the real world well after the retreat is over. Scott and Carmen Ramsey plan to join four couples, as well as their new buddy Jason Courtney, for next year's vacation. They're just that tight.

"It's all because of the relationships developed through Office Pride," Scott says.

More Information

If you would like more information on how you can clean up with this exciting franchise opportunity, you can call 727-777-6634 or visit https://officepridefranchise.com.

FASTSIGNS®
More than fast. More than signs.®

Y ou'll agree with me, I'm sure, that FASTSIGNS® is an amazing company for numerous accomplishments, but one in particular stands out: Military veterans get a 50 percent discount at FASTSIGNS, the largest discount afforded by any franchise company in the nation! Hooray for FASTSIGNS for giving America's veterans an opportunity to succeed as franchisees.

But what amazing quality attracts non-veterans as well as veterans to this seasoned company? How about the franchisee financing programs? Start-up franchisees can apply for financing through Franchise America Finance, and FASTSIGNS extends financing to franchisees through its own $6 million credit facility.

Of course, in the world of signage and visual graphics, FASTSIGNS continues to be a top-rated franchise opportunity year after year.

The company's average initial investment is as low as $178,207 for a franchise with a net worth of $250,000. Franchisees consistently report that FASTSIGNS treats them well, beginning with its FASTSTART program that extends reduced royalties for a franchisee's first year so they have more money to invest in marketing their business.

FASTSIGNS is a professional, highly valued franchise opportunity that appeals to everyone who's thinking about building a business that serves the business community. The next chapter provides more details, and if you're interested in this concept, you can request more information.

— Dr. John P. Hayes

FASTSIGNS: Turn Your Business Ownership Dreams into Reality

FASTSIGNS® is more than a franchise opportunity — it's the chance to be a part of an internationally recognized brand and the largest sign, graphics, and visual communications franchisor in North America.

FASTSIGNS is part of a $29 billion industry, in which its share is $446 million in systemwide revenue. Moreover, it is a great time to be a part of this thriving sector of franchising since the International Sign Association <u>has a strong, positive outlook</u> as the ongoing worldwide need for visual communications and digital signage technology continues to grow.

The world of signage and visual graphics is an exciting, rapidly expanding business, and FASTSIGNS continues to be a top-rated franchise opportunity. If you're seeking a business opportunity that offers you the chance to meet a growing demand for eye-catching graphics and marketing through franchising with an established brand with a proven business model, look no further than FASTSIGNS.

What You Need to Know about FASTSIGNS

Founded in 1985 in Dallas, Texas, FASTSIGNS International, Inc. is the worldwide franchisor of 660 independently owned and operated FASTSIGNS centers in eight countries, including the U.S., Canada, England, Saudi Arabia, the UAE, Grand Cayman, Mexico, and Australia, where centers operate as SIGNWAVE®.

FASTSIGNS locations provide comprehensive sign and visual graphic solutions to help companies of all sizes and across all industries attract more attention, communicate their message, help visitors find their way, and extend their branding across all of their customer touch points, including décor, events, wearables, and marketing materials.

But don't call FASTSIGNS a sign company. They're more than signs. As businesses look for better, innovative ways to compete with new media, FASTSIGNS capitalizes on this demand with products and services that extend well beyond the traditional to include digital signage, interior décor, and architectural signage.

FASTSIGNS' is more than a sign company, offering solutions designed to help businesses of all sizes.

Growing at Home and Abroad

Over the past two years, FASTSIGNS International, Inc., has signed more than one hundred new franchise agreements and opened more than eighty new, co-branded, and conversion locations throughout the United States and around the world, including its first location in Dubai — the first of twelve centers planned for the UAE. The brand also sold future development rights to include North Africa and the Caribbean, and continues to grow aggressively in Australia under the SIGNWAVE® brand, in the U.K., and across Canada.

Awards & Accolades

When we say FASTSIGNS is the best, we mean it. What sets FASTSIGNS apart from other businesses is the fact that they are the top sign and graphics franchise in the industry. Their franchisee mentor network, financing options, education programs, and 120+ support staff experts are all designed to make the company the best in the industry, as indicated by numerous awards and notable recognition — all of which has fueled the brand's immense growth over the last thirty-two years.

Most recently, FASTSIGNS International, Inc., was ranked #1 in the business services and signs category, and #95 overall, on *Entrepreneur* magazine's 2017 Franchise 500, the world's first, best, and most comprehensive franchise ranking. FASTSIGNS also was named the #1 franchise opportunity on Franchise Gator's "Top 100 Franchises" list in 2016 and 2017.

For the last eleven years, FASTSIGNS has achieved World Class Franchise certification — the highest honor bestowed by the Franchise Research Institute — and, in 2015, was one of the inaugural inductees to Franchise Business Review's Hall of Fame for being named to its "Top Franchises" list for ten consecutive years for our high rate of franchisee satisfaction. Franchise Business Review also ranked FASTSIGNS #1 in franchisee satisfaction in 2016 and we recently were named to its "Top Innovative Franchises" list.

FASTSIGNS CEO Catherine Monson with
St. Louis franchisee Steven Hill.

About FASTSIGNS CEO Catherine Monson

When you join FASTSIGNS, you can be certain you're getting one of the most dedicated and passionate leaders in franchising. Since CEO Catherine Monson joined FASTSIGNS International, Inc. in 2009, the brand has continuously been rated as a top franchise opportunity and has grown to 660 locations across eight countries.

Monson, who has more than thirty years of franchising and management experience, has received numerous awards and recognitions, including the International Franchise Association (IFA) Bonny LeVine Award for her contributions to the growth of the franchising industry.

In 2010, the *Dallas Business Journal* named her one of the top Women Industry Leaders in the Dallas Metroplex. Catherine also appeared on the Emmy Award-winning series "Undercover Boss" in 2012 to learn new ways to advance the FASTSIGNS brand.

In 2015, she received the International Franchise Association's first Franchise Action Network FAN of the Year award for her advocacy work in the franchising community. In 2016, she was selected as a Soderstrom Society Inductee for her contributions to the printing and graphic communications industry and was also honored with the 2016 Leadership Award from the Women That Soar organization.

Catherine currently serves on the Board of Directors of the IFA and was elected Secretary in 2017. Additionally, she serves on the Board of Directors for two franchise companies — The Learning Experience® and Brain Balance Achievement Centers — and another industry association, Idealliance.

Franchise Opportunities with FASTSIGNS

Monson recently told *Forbes* that her ultimate goal is to grow FASTSIGNS to 2,500 locations in twenty-five countries. So it's safe to say that FASTSIGNS has ample franchise opportunities, both domestically and internationally, with over four hundred markets slated for development across North America.

FASTSIGNS is targeting aggressive expansion nationwide in the U.S. and Canada while also seeking a master franchisee for the Quebec province in Canada.

Beyond North America, FASTSIGNS is targeting multiple regions for growth, including Mexico, Southeast Asia, Central and South America, Brazil, India, and the Middle East, as well as Caribbean islands like Barbados, Bermuda, Jamaica, and Trinidad and Tobago.

FASTSIGNS Investment

To open your own FASTSIGNS location, the total investment is between $182,329 and $267,520, which includes a $47,500 franchise fee. The minimum requirements for prospective franchisees include $80,000 in available capital and a $250,000 net worth.

FASTSIGNS is assisting its own franchisees through its FASTSTART program. This program gives you 50 percent off of your first year's royalties so that you can invest in the marketing and promotion of your new FASTSIGNS business location.

The per-center gross sales average for a full-service FASTSIGNS center is the best in the industry by far at $778,611.*

Financing Options

FASTSIGNS is a reputable franchise with a proven business model, which has equipped it to provide unmatched access to franchise funding for its franchisees. FASTSIGNS offers all franchisees powerful financing options, with over $21 million set aside just for financing in order to help franchisees fund their ambitions of owning a FASTSIGNS.

Veteran Incentives

For many veterans, transitioning out of service to daily civilian life can be difficult. FASTSIGNS is dedicated to helping veterans find success and purpose through its sign franchise opportunities, which is validated by the fact that more than 10 percent of its franchisees are veterans. The franchise has been recognized as one of the "Top Franchises for Veterans" by Franchise Business Review and as a top "Military Friendly Franchise" by G.I. Jobs. In 2016, FASTSIGNS was honored with the prestigious Secretary of Defense Employer Support Freedom

Award, the highest recognition presented by the Department of Defense to employers for their exemplary support of National Guard and Reserve members.

FASTSIGNS offers military veterans the most comprehensive support and financial incentives available in the signage industry. FASTSIGNS participates in the International Franchise Association's (IFA) VetFran program that provides military veterans with special incentives and assistance to open a franchise. Veterans can take advantage of specific incentives, including a franchise fee of $23,750 (a savings of 50 percent). FASTSIGNS is the only franchise in its industry to offer a 50 percent discount to any veteran, without stipulations.

Veterans Milton Guerrero and Woody Poole, both nuclear-trained chief petty officers in the U.S. Navy, co-own their FASTSIGNS franchise in North Charleston, South Carolina. The partners met while serving.

"We began looking at franchises and FASTSIGNS instantly stood out from the rest," Guerrero says. "We weren't just blown away by the business model – it was also the great resources and ongoing support they provide franchise partners."

If you're a veteran, ask for more information about FASTSIGNS' Veterans Program.

The FASTSIGNS concept is adaptable and versatile.

Co-brand Franchise Offerings

The beauty of a FASTSIGNS franchise is its adaptability and versatility in the 21st century. With the availability of the Internet, industries involving photography and print are slowly declining. As a leader in the signs and graphics industry, FASTSIGNS offers incredible advantages and sign franchise opportunities to individuals, including co-brand and conversion franchise offerings.

FASTSIGNS' co-brand franchise offerings allow owners of established, related businesses to add a FASTSIGNS center to expand their product lines and services, while benefiting from ongoing training and support from the franchise system.

Opportunities are available for just $15,000 down for the franchise fee, and layouts can fit into as little as 400 square feet of an existing business.

FASTSIGNS often co-brands with print shops, camera stores, trophy and engraving businesses, photo-processing companies, and embroidery shops — but the opportunities are endless.

When franchisees co-brand with FASTSIGNS, they immediately benefit from brand recognition, access to an ad fund that is more than 2.5 times greater than that of the next largest competitor, access to a nationwide network of franchisees, and access to top-of-the-line training and support.

FASTSIGNS franchisee Gaby Mullinax of of Fullerton, California, is a professional photographer and has owned Fullerton Photographics, a photo retail shop, since 1999. In September 2016, she decided to expand her business by co-branding with FASTSIGNS to provide customers the ability to stay on the cutting edge of the sign, graphics, and visual communications industry.

"As a woman business owner, I've found a true partner in FASTSIGNS, who will help expand my existing business by providing our new and current clients the ability to stay on the cutting edge of the sign, graphics, and visual communications industry," she says. "For businesses looking for ways to expand their current portfolio and increase their revenue in today's fast-paced market,

FASTSIGNS offers an opportunity, including training and support, that is first class in service and made the decision process easy for me."

Conversion Franchise Offerings

As a business owner, you know how challenging it can be to establish brand recognition and serve your local market. The FASTSIGNS conversion franchise offerings allow business owners to join an established brand with a proven business model and support system to help them successfully meet the needs of their business community. In fact, FASTSIGNS' allowance often covers much of the conversion cost. Reaching your full potential is easy when you join the #1-ranked sign franchise in the industry.

Suki Khansarinia of Pomona, California, is a first-time franchisee who has begun to convert her existing sign and visual communications business into a FASTSIGNS location.

"I absolutely loved the patience and guidance the entire FASTSIGNS team provided throughout the entire process of deciding which franchise opportunity to invest in," she says. "While choosing a new business venture is never easy, I required a lot of information and time before making the best decision for my family. Every person who stepped in to answer my questions made me feel comfortable and provided honest answers based on their personal experiences. I never felt pressured. The exceptional franchise support that FASTSIGNS offers to their network of franchisees helped them stand apart from our other options, and we truly look forward to joining the FASTSIGNS family."

Ownership Benefits: Lifestyle and B2B Relationships

Owning your own business is one of the most important decisions you will make in your lifetime. FASTSIGNS provides the information you need to make a smart decision by helping you tie your business goals to your personal goals.

Franchising is a rewarding path to self-employment that provides you more control over your professional and personal life. As a FASTSIGNS franchisee, you can find the right balance between work and family. FASTSIGNS franchisees appreciate B2B working hours with no weekends or evenings.

FASTSIGNS allows you to control your future as you become involved in your community as a visual communications solutions provider for business customers from all industries. FASTSIGNS franchise owners enjoy a lifestyle of managing a low number of employees and building business-to-business relationships. Clientele are professional businesspeople and owners. Other benefits include low staffing requirements and attractive margins.

Steven Hill of St. Louis, Missouri, became a FASTSIGNS franchisee in 2017 after spending twenty-five years working directly with businesses selling technology.

"The thing I really love is that FASTSIGNS gives you a lot of flexibility because there are different products you can sell under the FASTSIGNS umbrella," he says. "From banners and yard signs to channel letters, or anything to do with branding, marketing, and helping companies get better visibility — all of that is FASTSIGNS. I don't know if there's any other company that has such a unique offering. With the FASTSIGNS model, you're talking to business owners. And that was a very comfortable conversation for me. I love helping business owners maximize their value."

Training & Support

While FASTSIGNS is known among businesses as a quick and reliable signage and graphics provider, it is also known in the franchise industry for equipping its franchisees with the tools for success. More than 120 support staff serve over six hundred franchisees. That's a support ratio of 1:6, the largest of any sign and graphics franchise anywhere.

New franchisees receive extensive training opportunities to learn about business operation and the visual communications industry. They spend four weeks in training with one week in a local FASTSIGNS center, two weeks at FASTSIGNS International's Dallas headquarters, and one week of onsite training in their new center.

Additionally, every new franchisee is provided with a franchise mentor to guide them as they build their business.

FASTSIGNS franchisee Denise Acquaye of Newark, New Jersey, celebrated her fifth anniversary with the brand in 2017. She calls the decision to join FASTSIGNS "monumental."

"After forty combined years in Corporate America, my husband and I wanted to follow our hearts and become entrepreneurs," she says. "We knew franchising was the right path because it would provide us with a proven business model to be successful. We looked at a lot of different concepts, from fast food to retail, but realized that with FASTSIGNS, we didn't have to retool ourselves. Our professional backgrounds segued perfectly into owning this business. But the reason we picked FASTSIGNS was because of its strong commitment to supporting franchisees. Without any company-owned centers, FASTSIGNS' success is entirely driven by its franchisees — so the corporate team allocates an enormous amount of resources to support."

With continuous education opportunities like the FASTSIGNS University and sales training, franchisees are equipped to grow into being an industry leader in their region. Annual conventions and vendor shows, regional meetings, message boards, and a Franchise Advisory Council allow franchisees to engage with individuals in the FASTSIGNS community.

FASTSIGNS Cares

FASTSIGNS International, Inc., launched FASTSIGNS Cares, an initiative that blends local charity support, team building, and community involvement.

In FASTSIGNS Cares' inaugural year, franchisees across the U.S. and Canada chose a variety of organizations to assist, including local chapters of national charities and specific local charities, and by honoring returning servicemen and women with signs and banners.

"FASTSIGNS franchisees are people who care about people. We are proud of the ways that they serve their local communities and we look forward to expanding this initiative in the years ahead," says FASTSIGNS CEO Catherine Monson.

The need for the services offered by FASTSIGNS continues to grow.

Why You Should Choose This World-Class Franchise

FASTSIGNS has always remained on the cutting edge of its industry. Ever since first opening doors back in 1985, FASTSIGNS realized the need to continue growing alongside the industry if they wanted to stay profitable and successful. This commitment has allowed the franchise to develop into a highly adaptable company, providing visual marketing solutions that meet the ever-evolving needs of franchisees and clients.

The need and demand for signage and graphics continues to grow. Businesses are looking for new and innovative ways to compete for attention in a visually oriented world and, as a result, FASTSIGNS franchisees are in the perfect position to achieve long-term success by crafting creative, cutting-edge solutions for businesses on a local and global scale.

So why should you choose this world-class franchise? Because joining FASTSIGNS immediately broadens your horizons. Instead of struggling to stay relevant in a competitive industry, franchisees instantly join the #1 brand in the sign, graphics, and visual communications industry.

More Information

For information about the FASTSIGNS franchise opportunity, visit www.fsfastsigns.com, or contact Mark Jameson at mark.jameson@fastsigns.com or 214-346-5679. Follow the brand on Twitter @FASTSIGNS, Facebook at facebook.com/FASTSIGNS or on LinkedIn.

* Per FASTSIGNS 04.30.2017 Franchise Disclosure Document, (FDD) and other sign franchises that disclose sales information in their FDDs.

If you like being on top, then you'll like being a part of the Restoration 1 franchise network. In 2017 alone, *Entrepreneur* magazine ranked the franchise opportunity on the Franchise 500 list, the Fastest-Growing Franchises list, the Top Franchises Under $100K list, and the Top Franchises For Veterans list. These accolades help underscore why the network has grown from eighteen locations to more than 175 in the last couple of years.

Restoration 1 franchisees get the chance to be a hero every time they go to work because when customers call, they are experiencing an emergency, and Restoration 1 franchisees get to save the day. How many franchisees can say that?

The Restoration 1 franchise network includes former Wall Street employees, corporate executives, military veterans, retirees pursuing their second career, new college graduates, and even the brand's first female franchise owner. The typical qualities they all share include the desire to be the boss, their attraction to realizing a strong return on their investment, their appreciation of being a part of a growing national brand, and the forward-thinking of an exit strategy when they are ready to leave the business.

Restoration 1 franchisees reap the rewards of national vendor relationships, access to the best suppliers and services, a professional online presence, the design of professionally branded trucks and uniforms, a strong peer network, an experienced support team at corporate headquarters, and an industry with built-in demand. And, most of all, the Restoration 1 network epitomizes how dirty jobs pay well.

If you'd appreciate an amazing business in the $60 billion restoration industry, continue reading to learn more about Restoration 1.

— Dr. John P. Hayes

Finding Franchise Success in the $60 Billion Restoration Industry

Timing is everything, as the saying goes. Just ask Beth Hendriks, of Raleigh, North Carolina.

When a heavy storm sent a tree crashing through the roof of one of her rental properties, Hendriks managed the repairs to her rental home by herself. In the process, she encountered the frustrating experience and countless headaches of working with contract workers she hired to handle the repairs. She was able to complete the restoration project on her own, but she knew there had to be a better, more efficient way to do the job.

The disaster led Hendriks to a future in one of the fastest-growing franchise opportunities: Restoration 1. It was only a matter of time before she started providing a critical service to others in her community.

The timing was perfect because when the disaster struck, Hendriks also happened to be researching various franchise opportunities for a future investment. After years as a C-wing executive with a nice parachute to put toward a new venture, she came upon Restoration 1. And, like other corporate evacuees looking to transition from a corner office to be the boss in another lucrative field, she dove straight into the restoration industry.

"Going through the restoration process from a customer's point of view really opened my eyes to what customers want and need from a restoration company," Hendriks said. "When I found Restoration 1, they were already connecting all those dots, and I knew this was a business where I could excel."

Her business savvy zeroed in on a great company with superior customer service that would be perfect for her in a field that has an ongoing demand. Hendriks was ready to offer others a solution without all the headaches.

Some 14,000 people in the U.S. experience a water damage emergency at home or work each day. The annual cost to insurance companies from water and mold tops $2.5 billion each year. And a whopping 37 percent of homeowners claim to have suffered losses from water damage.

As CEO, franchise veteran Gary Findley has Restoration 1 on a strong growth path.

Rapid, Yet Steady Growth

Founded in 2008, Restoration 1 is an award-winning organization that specializes in fire, water, and mold remediation services. Franchisees also provide emergency and storm-damage services, sewage system cleanup and more. With locations across more than half the U.S. and a rapid yet steady pace of expansion, Restoration 1 has become one of the fastest-growing and most-trusted restoration franchises in America.

In addition, franchisees point to four key elements about the business that get them up and running quickly: recession resistant, low overhead, low investment level, and no brick-and-mortar location to get started.

Of course, that doesn't mean just anyone can do the work. As disaster restoration experts, Restoration 1 franchisees are professionally trained to step in and handle emergencies, no matter how big or small, at a moment's notice. Every second counts when dealing with property damage, so Restoration 1 franchisees are committed to helping customers preserve their property, including keepsakes inside their home or business, and getting the property owners back to their normal day-to-day as quickly as possible.

Getting Down and Dirty

Putting the "restore" into restoration is where customers' hang their hopes and expectations. To do that, Restoration 1 franchisees are certified by the Institute of Inspection and Indoor Air Quality Association (IAQA), and have a Cleaning and Restoration Certification (IICRC).

These certifications help give property owners confidence that their restoration project is being handled by fully trained professionals.

Restoration 1 franchisees are heroes when tragedy strikes. While it can be a dirty business, it's also a billion-dollar industry that gives Restoration 1 franchisees an incredible chance to shine.

As another popular saying goes, things will get worse before they get better. That's entirely true when a typical day on the job can include tearing out drywall, pulling up carpet, and removing cabinets to get to affected areas that need attention. But when Restoration 1 delivers on the brand promise and a 100 percent satisfaction guarantee, nothing compares to the peace of mind, appreciation, and loyalty of a happy customer whose life can get back to normal.

So, who exactly are those "typical helpers"? These award-winning franchisees are part of one of the fastest-growing franchises in North America and come from all walks of life.

When Beth Hendriks signed her franchise agreement in May 2017 to open multiple locations in the Raleigh, North Carolina area, she became Restoration 1's first female franchisee.

No stranger to breaking glass ceilings, she previously spent 27 years in the tech industry as one of a limited number of female executives with a computer science background. It was this background that also made her appreciate the technology infrastructure and support built into Restoration 1's franchise model, which helps her run the business.

This mom of six is clearly not intimidated by a male-dominated field. Enthusiastic and well-suited to take the restoration industry by storm, she is building a successful franchise business focused on giving her customers the experience she would have appreciated when restoring her own property.

Franchisees are not required to operate a brick-and-mortar location to get their business running, reducing the initial investment needed.

Age Doesn't Determine Success

Just like gender, age is no barrier to becoming a Restoration 1 franchisee. Today, across a growing network of franchisees, the organization is attracting retirees looking for a new project, corporate refugees escaping the trappings of Corporate America, and even recent college graduates making the transition from student to business owner.

Recent graduates Francisco Burciaga and Alfonso Masso literally crossed the stage to receive their college diplomas and moved straight into a new franchise territory, opening their own business together.

Meeting as sophomores at Baylor University, Burciaga and Masso made their way through the entrepreneurship curriculum in the school of business and soon realized that franchising was a perfect fit and an ideal avenue to help them achieve their entrepreneurial dreams.

"Graduation came around and you start asking yourself, 'What's going to pay the bills now?'" said Burciaga. "We definitely didn't want to give up on entrepreneurial dreams, but at the same time, a grassroots startup idea fresh out of college was incredibly risky."

What started as a typical friendship between former college roommates quickly transformed into a business partnership. Burciaga and Masso got advice from other franchisees on securing financing and were signing papers to become Restoration 1 franchise owners within a week of their college graduation.

"They all said just walk into a local credit union, tell them your story, tell them the story about Restoration 1. It was nice to be able to go in and shake the hand of the person approving the loan," said Burciaga. "It definitely helped to be a franchisee and to come in with some history—this is the CEO, this is what the average franchisee makes."

They jumped head first into training and completing their certifications. Soaking up all the experience and information they could during training, the pair set up shop by purchasing their first van. In no time, they were answering their first business call – a water-damage and mold-removal job.

Today, they are operating a thriving franchise in Austin, Texas, and celebrated their first business anniversary in the fall of 2017.

From Combat Boots to Work Boots

Retired military veterans also find a good fit with Restoration 1.

After spending 13 years in the military, Joey Buchino knew one thing for certain – he DID NOT want to work for anyone when he returned to civilian life. Buchino thought his military training in the U.S. Army had perfectly primed him for franchise ownership. Thanks to Uncle Sam and the discipline and leadership skills needed to serve in the Armed Forces, Joey learned the value of following a system. He found a similar system to follow in the business world with Restoration 1. As a participant in the VetFran program, Restoration 1 is one of the respected franchise organizations that offers discounts to veterans who want to purchase a franchise.

"I knew I wanted to be my own boss," said Buchino, who owns a franchise in Parkland, Florida. "I knew nothing about owning or running a business. So, I went into franchising with Restoration 1 because I knew that it would shorten my learning curve when it came to business."

While he didn't have any formal experience owning or running a business, the Restoration 1 franchise has proven to be a smooth transition as he traded in combat boots for work boots and began to get down and dirty in his own business.

While he may have traded in one uniform for another, Buchino wakes up every day and finds himself using skills he learned in the Army to lead his Restoration 1 teams on important and time-sensitive missions.

*Because natural and man-made disasters never take time off,
the restoration industry has proven to be recession-proof.*

Recession-proof Opportunity

What attracts so many franchisees from so many different walks of life to the Restoration 1 franchise network? Perhaps the biggest attraction is the opportunity to own a business in a $60 billion industry that is not only here to stay, but is increasingly in demand. Because disaster can — and often does — strike at any time, the restoration industry has proven to be recession-proof. Natural and man-made disasters don't take days off, which means restoration professionals experience a constant need for their services.

Another reason the demand for restoration services is expected to grow is because the majority of Americans are living in older homes, where mold and water damage has become an increasing problem.

The health consequences associated with mold, smoke, and fire damage are well known and must be addressed quickly and professionally.

An Affordable Opportunity, a Winning Team

One attractive feature of the Restoration 1 opportunity is that franchisees are not required to operate a brick-and-mortar location to get their business running. As a result, they benefit from low overhead startup costs. Restoration 1 franchisees can operate their business out of a van as they build clientele and revenue. They are able to add a physical location when they are ready and financially stable. As a result, Restoration 1 has become one of the fastest-growing and most-trusted restoration franchises in the country.

Keeping the brand on the fast track for growth is CEO Gary Findley, a veteran in the franchise industry with over 25 years of experience. He previously helped two other franchise chains grow to over 9,500 locations worldwide.

"I credit our phenomenal franchise sales team and a franchise opportunity that has attracted the most incredible prospects in my entire career of franchising," Findley said. "From Wall Street executives and corporate evacuees, to military veterans and successful entrepreneurs, we have the most qualified leaders joining our network."

Findley is committed to growing the Restoration 1 franchise brand, and his immediate goals include expanding to more than 500 locations nationwide as well as expanding internationally with an immediate focus on the Canadian and UK markets.

Helping to fuel the brand's growth is the recognition Restoration 1 receives on a local and national level. *Entrepreneur* magazine named Restoration 1 one of the fastest-growing franchises in its Fastest-Growing Franchise List in 2017 and catapulted the company from #396 to #96 on the Franchise 500 list based on its rapid success.

But it's not only the media paying attention. Restoration 1 customers from across the country are passionate about sharing positive experiences with friends, family, and social networks. Making a lasting impression on customers through excellent customer service in a time of need has helped spread the word and share the brand with new customers and potential franchisees.

Endless Opportunities on the Horizon

Like all successful franchise chains, however, Restoration 1 is not content to rest on its laurels. In 2017, the franchise introduced a content cleaning program. This gives franchisees an additional, optional business opportunity for franchisees who want to provide a total restoration solution for customers experiencing property damage or loss by also helping them with the contents within their property.

"The content cleaning program is an exciting opportunity for us as a brand and a great way for our franchisees to take on an additional revenue stream within their existing business," said Findley. "We continually look for ways to offer added value to our franchisees, and this is one example of going that extra step that not only delivers for our franchisees but also for their customers."

Additionally, Restoration 1's acquisition of bluefrog Plumbing + Drain® in 2017 offers further diversity and growth opportunities. Existing Restoration 1 franchisees can pair their restoration business with a plumbing franchise, providing a convenient one-stop shop for customers, further helping to ease and simplify their restoration experience.

"Our success continues to grow, and so do the communities that we serve to rescue customers from unthinkable disasters," said Findley.

More Information

Looking to get down and dirty with a Restoration 1 business of your own? Restoration 1 is looking for active and enthusiastic entrepreneurs. There are plenty of attractive and high-profile markets still available for growth. For more information, visit www.restoration1franchise.com or call 888-912-6450.

Sandler Training®

One day many years ago I got a voice mail from David Sandler, founder of Sandler Training, asking me to come and pitch him my marketing services. I quivered with fear. A colleague asked what was wrong and I said, "I just got a call from David Sandler, the sales guru, asking me to come and sell him on our marketing services."

"Great!" said my colleague, who looked at me curiously. "Aren't you excited?"

Sure, I was excited, but what did I know about selling? Pitching Sandler was akin to pitching an entire Shark Tank panel.

It turned out that I had nothing to fear because Sandler was mostly interested in hiring me to write his book, *You Can't Teach a Kid to Ride a Bike at a Seminar*, and I knew how to pitch a book. Nothing sells like a book. Well, maybe Sandler!

It turned out that Sandler was one of the most gregarious franchise founders. One of the highlights of my career was getting to know him and writing his book, which franchisees continue to use more than 20 years later!

I also enjoyed spending a few years working with Sandler and his team, including his protégé David Mattson, who is now CEO and president of Sandler Training with more than 265 franchisees.

Many of the Sandler Training franchisees that I met in the mid-1990s are still franchisees today.

"We have a very low turnover rate," explains Ron Taylor, who leads the company's franchise sales division. Taylor was also a member of the Sandler team in the mid-1990s. "Franchisees don't leave us because we give them their life back. They build a great business doing what they love to do but without the travel!"

If you love selling and helping other people excel in business, chances are you'll love discovering Sandler Training. You'll find opportunities for multiple income streams and recurring revenue, along with brilliant resources that will help you build your business. Keep reading!

*— Dr. John P. Haye*s

Sandler Training: The #1 Sales Training Franchise Organization in the World*

Tim Goering and Rochelle Carrington share their personal journeys as Sandler Training® franchisees

If your professional goals include achieving a better work/life balance and financial freedom, you're in sync with the two primary reasons people invest in a Sandler Training franchise. Sandler franchise owners brag about achieving the work/life balance that eluded them while climbing the corporate ladder, and they rave about the financial freedom they enjoy while building their Sandler® business.

By combining a leading training franchise organization with a successful sales system, Sandler has created opportunities for franchise owners in a multi-billion-dollar training market, utilizing a recurring revenue model. Today, there are 250 Sandler franchise offices worldwide providing sales and management training programs in fifteen languages!

Could there be a Sandler Training franchise in your future? Before you answer, consider the stories of franchisees Tim Goering in Jupiter, Florida, and Rochelle Carrington in suburban New York and Connecticut. Had you asked either of them if they could see themselves as Sandler franchisees while they were still climbing the corporate ladder, they would have said, "No!" In fact, Carrington said she would never buy a franchise because she didn't want to be "controlled," and Goering already had a plum position with a $500,000-plus income. But look at them today!

Marine Who's Now a Franchisee

Goering proudly acquired a Sandler Training franchise on November 10, 2014, the birthday of the U.S. Marine Corps. Of course he was a Marine and is still a Marine at heart. Shortly after his stint in the service, where he ran insertion and extraction, search and rescue and test pilot missions, he completed a Myers-Briggs personality profile.

As he recalls, "They told me, 'You're a sales guy,' and I said, 'No, I'm not!' Then they told me to find a sales job and I'd make $100,000 within a year. Turns out that was good advice. There's a lot of money in sales!"

One sales job led to another until Goering discovered his talent for networking with wealthy people. His Wall Street employer sent him to West Palm Beach, Florida, as a financial advisor, and even though he found the job intimidating, he said he followed the game plan and met the right people. In this case, the right people were folks with $25 million or more in investments.

As Goering continued climbing the corporate ladder, he spent several years as a regional bank president, and then became the managing director of wealth management for all of Florida, representing a popular national bank.

"I managed people in six offices across the state," he explains. "Our job was to find people with millions of dollars and convince them to invest their money with our bank forever. It was a sophisticated sale."

The Pain of Developing Talent

But the real challenge was not finding wealthy investors; it was finding the talent that could find the wealthy investors. "The people who were good at this job were earning $500,000 to $1 million annually," says Goering, "but our employee turnover rate was fifty percent." Any time Goering lost an employee, he felt the pain. "We easily spent $500,000 on a producer before we knew if they were going to make it, and when we lost one I had to accept some of the responsibility because I recruited them." However, the bigger issue might have been the sparse resources devoted to training and developing employees.

In fact, it was a desire for training and development that led one of Goering's "big producers" to hire a sales coach in Boca Raton, Florida. "My coach teaches a sales curriculum that was created by David Sandler and it's the best training I've ever had," the employee told Goering.

He had never heard of Sandler, but he was intrigued. He discovered Sandler's book, *You Can't Teach a Kid to Ride a Bike at a Seminar*, read it, and loved it.

"I didn't understand it all," he recalls. "No one could until you apply it and realize how valuable it is. But then I met the coach because I wanted to learn more about the Sandler Training business. Oh, my gosh, I discovered it is such a cool business plan!"

Shortly after his introduction to Sandler, Goering says he had a "light-bulb moment." He wondered why he should struggle to provide sales training to his employees when he could hire Sandler to do it better. Unfortunately, his superiors didn't see it that way.

The Value of Repetitive Training

"The bank wasn't going to invest in Sandler," he explains, "not because they didn't believe in it, but because they decided we should do our own proprietary training in-house. And we did. All two hundred advisors were trained for three days, but there was no repeat training, so there was no reinforcement," which is a huge part of the Sandler Training business plan, and a major reason for the success of Sandler's franchisees and their franchisees' clients.

After two years of watching while the bank's training program didn't produce the desired results, Goering decided to make a career change even though it meant forfeiting his impressive income.

"I was so in love with the psychology of the Sandler program that I decided to become a Sandler franchisee and train clients how to sell more effectively," he says.

He quit his job and bought a franchise, taking advantage of Sandler's discounted price extended to military veterans.

Why Goering Bought a Franchise

Prior to making this dramatic decision, Goering visited Sandler headquarters to attend a Discovery Day and "kick the tires." In the back of his mind, he was still thinking his bank might agree to provide Sandler training to all their advisors, but it never happened. And it was just as well.

"During the Discovery Day, I couldn't believe the content Sandler had developed for franchisees. I had been developing my own content for fifteen years, but Sandler had about nine hundred hours more material than I had. For the price of the franchise, it made no sense not to buy the business."

"Amazing" and "fantastic" are words that franchisee Tim Goering uses to describe the quality of training and support he receives from his franchisor.

To many people, however, the timing of the opportunity didn't make sense. Recently divorced and committed to paying out-of-state tuition for two children in college, Goering recalls, "It was the most expensive year of my life." But he saw that as an advantage. "I'll never have more money going out the door than now," he told himself, "so the timing is perfect to take all my savings and buy a franchise. I have no choice but to make it work."

The Marine admits to being scared! "I was scared the entire time," and his first Sandler coach (Sandler provides a coach to every franchisee) didn't help much. "He asked me why I bought the franchise. I said because it would be fun to help people and companies make more money."

And the coach said, "You're going to struggle in this business!"

A Sandler Coach Sets Him Straight

That's not what Goering wanted to hear, but he soon realized it was what he needed to hear. He also soon realized that his coach was using a Sandler technique to motivate him.

"Do you think someone making $500,000 a year needs your help?" the coach asked. "What are you going to tell him? That you'll help him make $550,000 a year?"

"My coach challenged me to think differently about the franchise," Goering explains. "The goal wasn't so much for me to help people as for me to discover with people how to help themselves through my training."

The coach also helped Goering set specific goals for developing his business.

The Right Business for You?

Nowadays, many prospective franchisees call Goering to ask if it's a good idea to buy a Sandler Training franchise. Of course Goering thinks it's a great idea, but "it's presumptuous to say it works for everyone," he adds.

"It's a hard business," says Goering, "and if you're the type of person who's going to worry about getting your website perfect or producing the greatest brochure before you go out and find clients, then this is not the business for you. You're not buying a Baskin-Robbins or a Dunkin' Donuts where everyone knows your brand and they'll stand outside the door the day you open. This is different. We sell selling. Most people don't know Sandler and you're going to ask them to pay you a great deal of money for your services. It's a sales business, and starting out you're the only sales guy."

The Most Rewarding Business

But, he says, it's also the most rewarding business! He loves his work/life balance.

"I spend fourteen hours a week training," Goering explains, and you can tell he relishes that opportunity. "I need to spend twice that time to prepare. The rest of the time I'm prospecting, making cold calls, warm calls (using his LinkedIn contacts) and attending networking events looking for new clients."

To him, every step is an adventure that adds meaning – not to mention value – to his life. He quickly adds that he does it all in four days a week, not five.

"I don't work Fridays," he explains. "It's an admin day for me."

It gives him time to catch up on paperwork, to read, or to do whatever he desires.

The worst part of his week, he says, is cold calling. It seems no one wants to make cold calls. Sandler says it's like putting your arm in a meat grinder!

"I network in order to reduce the number of cold calls that I have to make," explains Goering. "My goal is to get five business cards per networking event, and I know those people will take my calls when I follow up. If I can also get a referral from each one of them, that's all the better."

Embracing Absolute Freedom

Recently he worried that he was taking too much time off, but then his Sandler coach asked him, "Why'd you start your own business?"

"Freedom!" Goering announced.

"So now that you have it, why aren't you taking it?" The response made it easier for Goering to spend a week on Cape Cod.

Once he returned to Florida, he got back into action. "I wake up every day and I tell myself I'm going to reach out to ten people via phone and email. It's on my task list and I know I won't feel good about the day until I check that off."

Ultimately, his goal is to work with a team of associates to build his company. And he'd like sixty days of vacation annually!

"That," he says, "is absolute freedom!"

And for Goering, that's the only motivation he needs. He says he's fortunate to have found a business that provides him with all the content and support he needs to do what he enjoys most: Empowering people to help themselves.

At the Top of the Sales Game in New York City

Meanwhile, Rochelle Carrington's story is much different, but similar in that she's also doing what she enjoys most. A ten-year Sandler veteran, she's using her Sandler franchise to build a different type of business in suburban Connecticut and New York.

Her goal is to build a multi-million-dollar business, but she wants to contribute the least to the revenue line.

"I don't want to be the number one salesperson anymore," she explains. "I've got to get someone else up to speed to take that role. I want to step back and not be the doer but the runner of the business. I see myself as a strategist who figures out how to run the business. I'm no longer in the cold-calls business. It's not for me. I don't have the time for it."

Rochelle Carrington scoffed at the idea of owning a franchise,
but she's now building a multi-million dollar business

What's more, she doesn't want to devote as much time to training, either. She just wants to run the business, and contribute at the level she desires. Essentially, she wants to do what she wants to do when she wants to do it. And why not? Like Goering, she's got absolute freedom!

Ironically, all of this comes from a woman who scoffed at the mere suggestion of buying a franchise. What happened?

She was determined not to buy a franchise!

From the time she was twenty-one, Carrington was in sales. She spent sixteen years selling advertising for fashion magazines in New York City, and for most of those years she loved it. She was at the top of a glamorous game. She moved into senior management, earned a great salary, lived the good life, but then she crashed.

"I burnt out," she explains. "I was bored and felt that I could do the job in three days rather than five, and that was frustrating. Part of it was the way we were selling. We would pitch and we wouldn't win, and then we'd give away a lot of unpaid consulting and we'd negotiate the price even though these were brand-name magazines. Eventually I decided to start looking for a business of my own."

When she met a business broker who sold franchises, she said, "That's the last thing I want! I'm a smart, creative person and I can figure things out myself. I don't want someone telling me what to do."

But the broker asked her to keep an open mind. Carrington agreed, and soon thereafter the broker introduced her to several franchises.

"My personal bias against franchises came from the big corporate world where there were rules and politics," Carrington explains. "I wanted to be on my own in business and I didn't need someone telling me what to do at all times. I didn't want to give up my creativity. Look at McDonald's. They're all the same! I wanted to build the business that I wanted."

But by being open-minded, Carrington discovered that not all franchises are the same and it's important to find the right fit. She admits that was a huge learning curve.

When her broker introduced her to a franchised car wash, and a maid service, she had no interest.

"Those weren't good businesses for someone coming from a fashion magazine," she says.

But then the broker told her about Sandler Training and a similar sales franchise.

"I didn't think I wanted to do sales. I was sick of it," she explains, "but my husband said that sales and management were what I knew how to do, so I said I'd take a look."

Even so, she was still determined not to buy a franchise.

"I agreed to travel to Baltimore to visit Sandler because it was a short drive from my home and I could visit my brother, so it wouldn't be a wasted trip," she says. "But I had no intention of buying anything."

Sandler's popular book remains a key part of the franchisee's tool box.

The Genius Moment that Created a Franchisee

What she didn't realize was that Sandler had no intention of selling her anything she didn't want to buy. All Sandler planned to do was what Sandler does best.

"They went through a talk that they use to generate prospects," Carrington remembers, "and the talk explains the steps in their sales system. It was a genius moment, and I thought: 'I have to do this! It's incredible!' They understood why

I was burnt out on selling. It wasn't that I didn't like sales, it was that I didn't like the old-style selling that didn't work."

Weeks later she became a franchisee, but her transition into franchising wasn't easy.

"Getting started was torture," she says, "because I was used to a big corporate company with a lot of support, an admin assistant, a car and driver, a big expense account, and suddenly it was just me. I didn't even know how to set up an Excel spreadsheet. I had to do everything myself, and that was a challenge. I was spoiled."

She also had no network to prospect for clients. She had spent all her career in New York City, but now that she was working in the suburbs, closer to home, she didn't know anyone.

"I really didn't know what a chamber of commerce was," she says. "The small-business world was completely new to me."

Leaning on Sandler

On top of it all, she had to learn the Sandler system, and that took time, too.

"That was a bigger shock because I felt like I had a Ph.D. in sales and suddenly I had to go back to preschool to learn how to read and write. That was a big hit to my ego."

Nonetheless, she persevered, but mostly, she says, she leaned on Sandler. She set her ego aside and asked for help.

"One of the great things about Sandler is the quality of training and support they provide. It's amazing. They assign every franchisee to a coach and you can talk to your coach every day if you want. That's fantastic. Then there's the franchisee network. I've found you can call a twenty-year veteran and they'll spend an hour helping you by phone on any topic. All you've got to do is ask for help, and I asked all the time. I studied like crazy and eventually it all came together."

Once she was ready to go to work, she discovered that she preferred public speaking to making cold calls and networking, but she did it all.

"I'm action oriented," she explains, "and I had to be to make money."

She got her first big sale within forty-five days.

"I met the prospect at a Starbucks," she remembers. "I didn't discount the sale, and he gave me his credit card on the spot."

There was only one problem: She had yet to set up credit-card processing, so she couldn't collect the fee! Undaunted, she wrote down the credit-card information, went home and called her coach, and he showed her how to charge the card.

The Road to a Successful Business

From the outset, Carrington liked both selling and training, but she says it took her almost two years to feel comfortable as a franchisee. Of course, she couldn't afford to let her discomfort get in the way of earning money.

Now she spends her time selling new business, speaking, and training. Every week she trains groups of clients at least twice, teaching them the Sandler Selling System, and she conducts in-house training, too, about a dozen times a month.

As she approaches her tenth anniversary as a Sandler franchisee, her immediate goals have changed.

"I'm going to hire someone who will take over a lot of the training, and I'm going to hire an additional salesperson to generate revenue. Ultimately I'll need three salespeople and me to build the company I want."

Still Feeling Creative?

But what happened to her creativity, which she didn't want to sacrifice to a franchisor?

"It still exists," she says and laughs. "It's important to find a franchise that fits you personally, and that's why Sandler is perfect for me. Sandler gives franchisees a base model and we can create the business we want. They gave me the clay and the basic structure of the body and I get to decide the hair color, eye color, size of the muscles, etc., and I love that about Sandler!"

To people who are interested in a Sandler Training franchise, both Goering and Carrington offer some advice. Carrington says it's important to consider the support a franchisor provides.

"When someone else has a good model, there's no need to recreate it. That will take too long and cost you too much money, and those are reasons to buy a franchise. But it's important to be sure the franchisor will support you, and Sandler does that better than any company."

Goering adds, "Don't blow off the training! Lots of times franchisees, for whatever reason, decide they're going to recreate the business. Sandler has already figured it out and all you have to do as a franchisee is attend the training programs that are offered throughout the year. Do that and you'll quickly learn how to master the business."

More Information

If a Sandler Training franchise sounds like a good idea for you, contact Ron Taylor at 800-669-3537, or visit their website at SandlerFranchising.com.

* — As ranked by 2016 *Entrepreneur* magazine

There's an amazing story behind the founding of LIME Painting, a franchise concept that appeals to people who want a home-based business in the high-end service industry. Company founder Nick Lopez didn't set out to establish a franchise business. He was a college student who needed money to cover the cost of tuition, books, and living expenses. That's when he accidentally discovered franchising.

Lopez left his home in Colorado to study business at Michigan State University. To earn extra money, he decided to start a business. Of course, he needed a business that would allow him time to study, and since he didn't have much money to invest, he needed an idea that wouldn't require much start-up capital. That's when he settled on painting . . . as in painting houses . . . especially million-dollar-plus houses.

While he knew little about painting houses, he knew how to treat people, and when he discovered that homeowners, especially wealthy homeowners, struggled to find dependable painters, he decided to meet that demand. Almost immediately he heard people thanking him just for showing up! These seemingly common practices were rare in the painting contractor world.

Within a short time, word of mouth boosted Lopez's business and he relied on painting houses to pay for college. By the time he graduated and returned to his home state, he knew he had a business that he could continue, no matter where he lived. Then it occurred to him that if he could make a business out of painting houses, so could others, especially with his leadership. And that's when the LIME Painting franchise was born.

If you'd rather manage a business that you own instead of operating your own business, you need to know about LIME Painting. You will have to master the business before you can step out of it to manage it, but ultimately you can own and manage multiple territories of this emerging brand.

LIME Painting is a Christian-focused organization that is driven by culture and values and uses for-profit business as a means to accomplishing mission. The following chapter tells you more about Lopez's story and his desire to help others with a mission to accomplish their goals through franchising.

— Dr. John P. Hayes

Franchisees Love to "Get Limed"

Lime Painting, LLC is a high-end residential and commercial interior-and-exterior paint company that delivers reliable, consistent, quality service. Customers enjoy an easy and refreshing turnkey service like no other. Lime Painting's residential target market includes homes valued at $1 million-plus, as well as custom commercial properties such as restaurants, resorts, retail locations and golf clubs whose paint needs include custom finishes like lacquer, faux, stain, glaze, and more. Lime is the only national specialty paint company that services markets like these.

Timing is Everything

Lime Painting is an amazing home-based franchise system within the specialty-paint service industry, and timing is everything for this cutting-edge concept. Working with an emerging franchise concept means having direct access, mentoring, and training from Founder and CEO Nick Lopez Sr., who presents a unique franchise offering and training skill-set. Beyond Lopez's rich understanding of the business, he is also a certified franchise executive, a designation awarded by the International Franchise Association.

Lime Painting began offering franchises during the latter part of 2017. The initial expansion strategy is to scale across the Southwest and outwards from corporate headquarters in Denver, Colorado, with an objective to expand to areas that allow for efficient travel. This way, franchisees can receive punctual and quality training from the corporate office.

The Lime Painting Franchise

The Lime Painting opportunity would be a perfect fit for franchisees who are looking for a service business that allows them to perform at a very high level in a recession-proof market. At all times – even in an economic downturn – home improvements are necessary. The Lime Painting franchise system operates within the robust home-improvement and repair sector, which touted well over $300 billion in annual sales during 2017 with 6.7% growth. Harvard University published the Leading Indicator of Remodeling Activity indicating three-year projections for growth to continue within the Home Improvement sector.

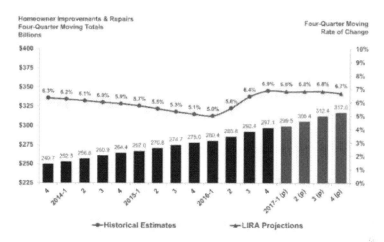

The training, processes, and systems at Lime Painting are top-notch game-changers that prepare franchisees to be successful within the home-improvement and repair sector. Quite frankly, Lime Painting is pioneering the way that customers in the high-end custom painting world perceive what it means to take on a home-improvement and painting project. Franchisees who are looking for a quality, home-based concept that has an investment level between $120,000 and $160,000 need look no further than Lime Painting.

With a concept that is very rewarding, Lime Painting franchisees can build relationships and serve an affluent customer base while solving challenging projects. Doing so requires a rich understanding of communication, customer service, service expertise, and ethics. Beyond being able to work directly with Lime Painting's founder, franchisees who enter the system early will be positioned for a potential spot on the influential advisory and founder boards. These roles contribute to brand strategy and initiatives, as well as represent the voices of Lime Painting franchisees.

Until franchisees master the business, Lime Painting is an owner/operator model. From there, franchisees can step back within their business to actively manage their location. Once on established footing, there is potential for franchisees to acquire other territories and scale those locations as a part of their portfolio. Lime Painting is set up for multi-unit operators and regional developers.

Risk and Reward From the Start

Some of the greatest discoveries happen by luck and others out of survival, but some of the best discoveries happen from a combination of the two. For instance, take Nick Lopez Sr.'s story. In 2009, at the peak of the housing crash and financial crisis, the beginning of a childhood dream was brought front and center. The reality of making that dream come true required grit, savvy, and a competitive will to win. The fear of failure became a powerful motivator.

At the time, Lopez's childhood dream of becoming a CEO seemed distant, but what stood imminent was the adversity dressed as a financial challenge in paying for an out-of-state education at a major university. As a financially independent and first-generation student, these cards set the stage for what would shape and mold Lopez's college journey. As an ambitious eighteen-year-old with a heart set on going to college – but with no financial means – it seemed very logical to pay for Michigan State University by walking onto the wrestling team in hopes of eventually earning a scholarship. Fate had a different plan, and this is Lopez's story.

Getting accepted was just the start. With no funds to get to Michigan from his home state of Colorado, Lopez charged a one-way flight on his first credit card. With a five-foot bag packed and holding all his belongings, Lopez ventured off to earn a business degree, which was the first of many steps to accomplishing his dream.

After becoming a preferred walk-on for the Michigan State wrestling program, Lopez struggled to pay for basic necessities, books, housing, and tuition. His grades took a back seat to financial and athletic demands. It soon became apparent that an athletic scholarship was at least a couple of years away, so Lopez hung up his wrestling shoes and picked up a paint brush. It was the first of many sacrifices that he made to make his dream become reality. Lopez would have to leave his most fulfilling childhood passion to find his calling.

Working with Lime Painting means direct access, mentoring, and training from Founder and CEO Nick Lopez Sr., (left) and his team.

Luck Complements Survival

At the time, operating a painting company was a great way to make more than he could ever hope to earn working at the dorm cafeteria. So Lopez founded Spartan College Painters, an East Lansing-based painting company, which serviced a high-end demographic. With quality in mind and an ear for customer requests, Lopez's goal as a home painter was to do for others as he would want done for him. In a short period of time, he began to hear, "Thanks for showing up," and, "Thanks for doing a good job," and "Thanks for being responsive." What seemed like common practice was actually rare in the world of painting contractors.

Time and again, Lopez's customers told him horror stories about previous painters. These tales of woe would soon become the driving force behind solving an industry-wide problem. Once Lopez began taking business classes in his third year of college, he learned about competitive advantage. At last, the light bulb went off. Out of a sheer will to survive, hard work, a willingness to serve, and a little luck, he stumbled upon a massive need in the market. All along, customers rooted for him and encouraged him; they saw him as the solution. Once Lopez realized how well customers accepted him, he became more passionate about giving back to the market that showed him the way to business success.

After two years of working in the industry, it was clear that Lopez had a compelling competitive advantage. However, working hard and doing a good job wasn't enough for him. Once he decided to pursue the industry head on, it was his sole focus to challenge the status quo within an industry that had set the bar low.

From Classroom to Real World

While Lopez sat in lecture halls and worked on his business degree, he was able to apply in the field what he was learning in the classroom. This from-the-lab-to-the-field approach was improved upon by direct customer feedback, which helped Lopez refine a desired customer experience. Looking at the big picture, Lopez's time working in the business alongside painters on ladders, paintbrush in hand, allowed him to understand the business from the customers', employees', and business owner's points of view. This unique vantage point became a powerful influencer that still guides Lopez's decisions today.

During his fourth and fifth year in business, Lopez was able to reflect on his paint business' overall success. His company's reputation began to open doors as influential customers helped him tap into a wide network within the community. This allowed Lopez to meet some of the Who's Who within the real estate development world. He began rubbing shoulders with developers who were building and shaping the city. Not only did he begin to do business with these developers, but these real estate gurus became mentors and advisors, too. Their wisdom contributed to what would become the Lime Painting strategy.

Proof is in the Painting

After five successful years in Michigan, Lopez moved back to Colorado to establish Lime Painting with an objective to assess the labor force, gain some market exposure, and validate that the model would adapt to new surroundings.

With one hundred jobs completed that first year, Lopez began hiring a team to continue the expansion of Lime Painting within the Denver market.

That effort, in addition to a second location that opened in Boulder in year four, resulted in $5.5 million in sales revenue and $1.3 million in gross profit in Lime's first four years. Lopez's goal was not to grow quickly but rather to keep up with demand while expanding in a responsible manner – with national expansion as the guiding compass.

Along the way, it was Lopez's objective to ensure that the model could take on market demand while maintaining quality, customer satisfaction, and a strong company culture. To date, those objectives have held true. After nine years of refining the model, Lopez is bringing Lime Painting to the franchise world.

The Problem with Superman

Lime Painting's strategy is straightforward: Raise the status quo within the painting world, an otherwise fragmented one-man show, or as Lime Painting coined it, "The Superman Model." Comprised of many hard-working people who are stretched too thin, the Superman Model struggles because of limited resources and a lack of processes and systems to provide consistent service.

This approach paved the way for how not to service high-end clients. By listening to customers' needs and what they didn't like about the industry, Lime Painting was able to build a solution-driven model with customer experience at the forefront.

Most one-man shows within the industry want to do a good job. However, they are unfortunately victim to what they don't know: business. Unethical behavior has also tainted the industry. Poor business etiquette has manifested itself into customer horror stories, such as "I can't believe he took my deposit and never did the work," or "The bill keeps growing even though I signed a contract for the scope and price," or "They showed up to my house to start the job and dropped off their equipment but haven't returned for weeks to complete the work." This mind-boggling list goes on and on. And that's why high-end homeowners are in dire need of a solution to the Superman dilemma.

*Lime Painting's reputation has spread quickly
in the world of high-end painting.*

Get Limed — The Amazing Solution

The ability to deliver a consistent, reliable, and quality paint service as promised is doable because of Lime Painting's model, which includes building teams with roles and quality controls. Lime Painting strives to exceed expectations by providing quality preparation, quality products, custom results, and lasting impressions. As the remarkable yet rare "purple cow" within the world of high-end painting, Lime Painting's solid reputation spreads quickly via word of mouth.

Lime Painting has capitalized on the market's long-overdue solution to customer frustration by winning lifelong relationships with customers who love to "Get Limed." Lime Painting brings customers and craftsmen together in a seamless approach. In a high-end market where custom-coating solutions are standard, Lime Painting must provide additional restoration expertise in order to leave a lasting impression. For customers, one of the best parts of "Getting Limed" is its turnkey approach – from first interaction to last brushstroke.

Lime Gives Back

Lime Painting's accomplishments are a direct reflection of what it stands for: Love, Integrity, Mission, and Excellence. These core values are personified in Lime Painting's social outreach – Lime Light Outreach, a 501(c)(3) nonprofit – and tailored to the youth in the communities that Lime Painting calls home.

The custom-paint service believes in giving back to the communities that have contributed to their success. For Lopez, establishing a nonprofit that provides a vehicle for each franchisee to connect with and improve its community is a win-win, and what better way to do so than to empower each community's youth?

Lime Light Outreach's three core competencies include raising funds, building awareness, and networking. Bringing awareness and knowledge while empowering youth through funding campaigns is presented through Lime Light's four pillars of awareness: faith, family, patriotism, and prosperity.

Lime Light's model provides for a way to give back with minimal resources and time invested on behalf of franchisees. Lime Light is the brains and funds behind a message that is orchestrated by established nonprofit partners.

Lime Painting franchisees deliver exceptional service to their customers.

The "It" Factor

Many companies are only able to deliver the bare minimum to their customers. But companies like Lime Painting that truly deliver an amazing, quality experience are the winners. It's the "it" factor, or a positive experience that satisfied clients refer to as "Getting Limed."

Today's savvy consumers not only want to do business with a trustworthy company that offers exceptional service, but they also want to build a relationship that goes beyond a basic business transaction. Lime Painting willingly takes on that challenge by relishing its role as a change agent within the communities it serves.

Lime's local commitment is threefold: creating jobs, leaving a lasting impression, and giving back through its Lime Light Outreach.

Why get Limed?

The Lime Painting train has left the station and is headed on an exciting journey. The great news is that potential franchisees can still jump onboard. You can be a pioneer of what is shaping up to be a game changer in a solution-seeking industry. As the saying goes, sometimes it's better to be lucky than good. If you think you have what it takes to perform at a high level and you are inspired by a strong, high-quality service culture, Lime Painting could be your once-in-a-lifetime opportunity.

You not only get the opportunity to run a successful business, but you also can be a part of making the world around you a better place. Join the Lime-green team and discover how we are lucky enough to work in beautiful places with beautiful people. Choose to Get Limed; you'll love it.

More Information

Are you interested in Getting Limed? If a colorful career move with a Lime Painting franchise sounds like a stroke of genius, call 720-708-7807 or visit www.limepainting.com.

zerorez.

Before Zerorez, the founders of this innovative franchise concept managed apartment buildings and spent a lot of money replacing carpets. Even after hiring a crew to clean carpets, they noticed that the carpets seemed to get dirty faster. Ultimately, they would have to replace the carpets to make an apartment presentable. But then they created Zerorez!

There are two amazing components of Zerorez. First, the company uses patented technology to clean carpets. If that sounds like just another sales pitch, give me a moment to explain. If you've hired a crew to clean a carpet, you have one of two methodologies: flood and suck, or spit and shine.

One method floods the carpet with water and chemicals (i.e., soap) and the other spins the water and chemicals into the carpet. Both processes extract the water and chemicals, but never entirely. In fact, the residue that's left in the carpet attracts dirt faster than before the carpet was cleaned.

Zerorez developed a new methodology that's disrupting the decades' old carpet-cleaning industry. The Zerorez process uses patent-protected "empowered water" (a machine attaches electricity to water) that cleans better than detergent and then evaporates, thus eliminating the residue problem. Zerorez also uses a patent-pending extraction process that rinses the carpet from bottom to top and prevents water from soaking the carpet padding. This process removes more of the water and speeds up the drying process.

The second amazing component of Zerorez is the franchise network. Of course, amazing franchise networks are not unique, but in any business it's a huge advantage to be associated with like-minded operators who collaborate to help one another succeed. Like other franchise networks, Zerorez franchisees look out for each other and, through their collaboration, contribute to a successful brand.

The Zerorez process not only cleans carpet but other surfaces, too, including tile, granite, hardwood, and air ducts. The company says, "If you live on it, sleep on it, eat on it, or walk on it, we can clean it!"

If Zerorez sounds like a franchise opportunity of interest to you, you'll learn more about the business in the next chapter. Then it's just a matter of requesting the company's free information.

— *Dr. John P. Hayes*

ZEROREZ ...The Right Way to Clean!

Carpet cleaning...sexy, right?! Nope, most people don't give it much thought, either as a service or a business. But what if you could own a business with superior customer retention and highly predictable margins with a completely differentiated model in a fragmented and commoditized market? Welcome to Zerorez!

The Zerorez Way is based on the idea that being invited into a client's home just once will win you a customer for life. That means you have the potential for recurring revenues without repetitive customer acquisition costs.

The carpet cleaning industry has gone largely unchanged since the 1940s, but Zerorez has introduced an innovative approach that is light years ahead of the competition.

Almost all carpet cleaners are still using the exact same, decades-old methods that were used to clean carpets during World War II. Most carpet cleaners today use one of three cleaning methods. First, there's what is called the "flood-and-suck" method; second, the "spit-and-shine" method; and then there's the less popular process called "encapsulation," or "leveling"—which we like to call "a huge cover up."

"Flood-and-suck" cleaners literally flood carpets with soapy water, completely soaking the carpets and often the padding and the floor beneath it. They then try to suck it all out again, with very little success. That's why it takes so long to dry, and when it does, most of the mess they were supposed to get rid of "magically" re-appears. It's called "wicking," and it's terrible!

The "spit-and-shine" cleaners aren't any better. All they do is slather carpets with nasty chemicals and smear them around with a spinning bonnet! While the carpet may dry faster, these cleaners just spread the mess around.

The "cover up" method is probably the worst of the three.

Dry chemicals, designed to trap dirt and oils, are scattered all over the carpet, and then brushed, wiped, or—in theory—vacuumed out. Really, they've only added more "stuff" to the carpet (including nasty chemicals).

Zerorez franchisees are in demand because of
a patented process that leaves no residue.

The Need for a Better Mousetrap

The underlying problem with every one of these methods is residue. A product, like a soap or a harsh chemical, is introduced to the carpet to make the dirt and oils easier to remove.

But once the product is attached to the carpet fibers, it's impossible to remove all of it, leaving a chemical residue behind. And since these products are designed to attract and hold onto dirt, those left behind become little "dirt magnets," which means the carpet will only get dirtier faster.

What if there was a system that didn't introduce those "dirt magnets" during the carpet cleaning process, a system that created "Zero Residue"? Well, for a lucky few franchise owners, there is!

Zerorez franchisees use a patented process to clean the right way with EMPOWERED WATER™. The process takes tap water and transforms it into a super-charged solution with extraordinary cleaning power. It dissolves dirt and oil on contact, like a soap or detergent, making them easier to remove, but without leaving the "dirt magnets" behind. The ZrLIFTER™ uses counter-rotating brushes to dislodge hair, dead skin, allergens, and deeply embedded dirt from carpet fibers that even industrial vacuuming cannot. The patent-pending ZrWAND™ uses a 180° loop spray to completely rinse the carpet fibers from bottom to top, effectively removing hard-to-reach dirt and debris without flooding the carpet.

As a result, Zerorez franchisees are able to recover 95 percent of the water put down. The result is a more thorough clean and a significantly faster dry time.

The Birth of Zerorez

The idea for Zerorez was conceived by co-founders Gaylord Karren and John Hopkins in the early 1990s while they were managing several thousand rental properties in Houston and Dallas.

Second only to payroll, the largest expense each month was the cost of replacing carpets. Their properties included more than 2.5 million sq. ft. of carpet, and every time a tenant moved out, the carpets had to be cleaned for the next tenant. Unfortunately, no carpet cleaner was able to clean the carpets well enough to avoid replacing them. As a result, Karren and Hopkins were spending over $100,000 every month just to replace carpets.

"There must be a better way," they thought, so they started researching available options only to discover carpet cleaning was an antiquated industry, ripe for innovation.

They set out to create a way to effectively clean carpet the right way, by not leaving dirt magnets behind. From their experience in the oil and gas industry, they knew of a technology that increased the pH of tap water until it acted like a cleaning agent but without leaving a residue. This was critical for flushing pipelines where various fuels were transported since it was critical that one fuel not contaminate another.

Transforming this technology to a vehicle-mounted delivery platform revolutionized a stagnate industry and created the path to a revolutionary way to clean...Zerorez! In a service sector that was mature and technologically stagnant, Zerorez now stands out as an innovator and a disruptive force for positive change.

In 2002, Karren and Hopkins launched their franchise program as they continued to perfect their business model. The early years were filled with exciting developments along with some frustrating challenges that needed to be overcome. The founders brought in two new partners who helped them create the only patented concept in carpet cleaning capable of addressing the pervasive issues with residue. They coupled it with an unparalleled service culture and have now expanded to over 40 markets in the U.S., approaching $100 million in systemwide sales.

Now they plan to begin an aggressive international expansion while continuing to march across the U.S., establishing regional developers and individual owner/operators in the Zerorez family.

Carpet cleaning is a $5 billion sector of the economy.

An Amazing Opportunity

According to the Carpet and Rug Institute, fifty-one percent of homes in the U.S. have carpet. That's an enormous pool in which to fish with a patented process, proprietary mobile unit, and an unparalleled approach to attracting and keeping customers. No current carpet cleaning service has over 3 percent of the market. The largest contingent by far is independent operators with no brand across markets, unproven systems and processes, no corporate backing for warranty, and no real commitment to even be in business next year!

The best-known brands continue to resell the same customers with an outdated model, inferior cleaning methods, and no real value proposition other than discounts and promotions. The incredible opportunity for Zerorez franchisees is an endless supply of customers who are fed up with "bait and switch" tactics, including the "hard-sell" of services they don't need. Once these customers experience the Zerorez Way, they are never going back!

Now that you've wrapped your head around the incredible size of the market for carpet cleaning, consider this: The Zerorez system works on tile, hardwood floors, granite countertops, upholstery, and vehicle interiors. The system also works on commercial applications, in office buildings, entertainment venues, schools, churches, and a myriad of other facilities. A relationship with Lifetime Fitness is an example of growing commercial business for Zerorez, and franchisees are uncovering new opportunities almost daily.

A Business Model that Works for You

Why would you want to launch a business where you have to continuously "sell" the same customer over and over by spending an exorbitant amount of dollars on marketing and then offering an endless barrage of discounts and promotions? Rather, why not get invited into a customer's home and "take them off the market"...that's the Zerorez Way!

Highly trained and motivated Zerorez technicians are absolutely crazy about clean. When they enter a first-time customer's home, they follow a carefully choreographed process to ensure that customer will never consider letting anyone or any other company touch their carpets, tile, hardwood, or other surfaces.

Consider the "water test," for example. A technician places the customer's own tap water in a jar and adds iodine. You can imagine what that looks like: a murky solution that is not too appealing. Then, placing Zerorez Empowered Water in a jar and adding even more iodine, the technician gently swirls the container and the iodine virtually disappears right before their eyes! The jar has crystal-clear water in it because the Empowered Water so efficiently breaks down the iodine you can't even see it.

This graphic display of how the Zerorez Empowered Water cleans reinforces the brand's unique approach to clean.

Next, technicians place an in-line filter on the extraction hose to show customers what is coming out of their carpet before they Zerorezify it. The typical

111

display is described by customers as "dirty, soapy coffee." Yet, once the technicians have performed the clean and reattached the filter, the resulting display is startling. Customers cannot believe the difference, further reinforcing that only Zerorez knows the right way to clean.

A Tiered Approach to Expansion

The top fifty-one markets in the U.S. are reserved for Zerorez Regional Developers — operators who want to dominate — like the Minneapolis franchise that dispatches more than fifty vans every day, or Atlanta that has more than forty vans in production, or Dallas, with more than thirty vans on the streets.

Regional Developers capture market share from local independent competitors, as well as national brands, by providing a superior process, high-quality service, and showing customers a "better mousetrap." These highly talented franchisees are actively marketing through top-talent radio endorsements, strong social media campaigns, and local television appearances by educating consumers about the right way to clean.

Ray Kennedy, Regional Developer and Owner of Zerorez Indianapolis, was attracted to Zerorez "because of the differentiated customer positioning, high gross margins, and strong service model." He plans on opening additional locations in his territory.

Franchisees can start with a single van and expand to meet market demand.

In addition to Regional Development markets, there are thousands of markets with less than a million in population that are available for a local franchisee, starting with one van and growing to meet market demand. Jeremy McGee in Spokane, Washington, population less than 500,000, started his Zerorez franchise a few years ago with a single unit. Today, he sends out sixteen technicians daily to serve his market, generating over $3 million in top-line sales.

"I am amazed at how quickly I was able to take over my market," says McGee. "Once customers experience Zerorez, they aren't willing to let anyone else in their home."

You might be thinking, "I know nothing about carpet cleaning."

Don't worry, you don't need to! New franchise owners benefit from outstanding technical and business management training to help learn the business quickly and effectively (no matter their background).

The support network includes experienced professionals in marketing, operations, training, and development, as well as experienced franchise owners who are willing to share their strategies and insight.

Anthony Holmes, owner of Zerorez of Puget Sound, had been looking into various businesses and franchises for several years before deciding on Zerorez.

"Not only was I impressed with the patented technological advantages and the strong commitment to service, I really felt like the corporate team put together a strong training program to get me up the learning curve as fast as possible," he said. "Since I had not been in the industry before, I needed a full program, from being on the van to answering calls to managing all aspects of the business. The corporate team went above and beyond to get me what I needed."

Now Zerorez is ready to launch its global expansion, and is already considering master franchisee partners for Australia, the Netherlands, the United Kingdom, and Canada. Anywhere with flooring and other surfaces that need to be cleaned the right way creates an amazing opportunity to replicate the success that Zerorez is experiencing in the U.S.

The Zerorez master franchisee in these global markets will enjoy access to the proprietary processes and trade secrets of Zerorez, including Empowered

Water, the ZrLifter and the ZrWand. This is a ground-floor opportunity for the right candidates to revolutionize the carpet cleaning industry in their country.

More Information

If you are ready to clean up on your share of the $5 billion carpet cleaning sector of the economy, then contact Zerorez today at 801-443-1034 or franchising@zerorez.com. Better yet, visit www.zerorezfranchising.com and submit your application to become part of the Zerorez family.

If you're searching for a "sweet" franchise opportunity, look no further than the next chapter, which provides details about River Street Sweets•Savannah's Candy Kitchen. This business is an all-encompassing sweets store where all of the confections are prepared in front of customers.

No other candy store makes more sweets than River Street Sweets, where customers fall in love with pralines, chocolates, fudge, loggerheads (chocolate turtles), caramel apples, popcorn, and homemade ice cream and gelato. These products are made every day while customers look on with admiration. The stores also feature a huge novelty hard-candy selection.

River Street Sweets is a family-run franchise business, and family members say it's an amazing business because:

- "Our World Famous Pralines are the best you will ever taste.
- We are in the business of making people happy. The candy business is one in which every guest leaves happy and with a smile on their face.
- We have a proven process, which has been tested for over 40 years.
- We are family owned and, as a franchisee, you become part of our family, with direct access to the founders.
- We are deeply committed to helping our franchisees grow their business."

So if you seek an amazing as well as sweet franchise business to own and operate, River Street Sweets•Savannah's Candy Kitchen may be perfect for you. Keep reading and then ask for information about this franchise opportunity.

— *Dr. John P. Hayes*

River Street Sweets•Savannah's Candy Kitchen
Stirs up Sweet Success

If you want to feel like a kid in a candy store, step inside River Street Sweets•Savannah's Candy Kitchen.

This unique franchise, which specializes in handmade Southern candies, is specifically designed to take you back to a sweet place filled with homemade desserts served with old-fashioned Southern hospitality.

The River Street Sweets•Savannah's Candy Kitchen experience is the opposite of what you'll find in a typical mom-and-pop candy shop. These stores offer an amazing interactive experience where the candy and other delicious treats are made right before your eyes. The business is not only about selling candy but also showing how it's been made for the past 40-plus years.

While guests shop, candy chefs are busy at work creating World Famous Pralines®, caramel and chocolate Loggerheads®, hand-stretched peanut brittle, glazed pecans, saltwater taffy, fudge, chocolate-covered strawberries, caramel popcorn, handmade ice cream and gelato, assorted hard candies, and a long list of other scrumptious treats. The stars of the show stir up delicious batches of pralines bubbling in copper kettles, hand dip them on marble slabs, and invite guests to taste a sample. How's that for a truly "sweet" business?

"There's nothing like a hot praline coming off a marble slab," said Tim Strickland, who co-owns the franchise brand with his sister, Jennifer Strickland, and their father, Stan Strickland. "It's the best dessert you'll ever have in your life."

Not a Fledgling Franchise

The River Street Sweets•Savannah's Candy Kitchen concept isn't a new, one-hit franchise wonder that has yet to prove itself. In fact, the established business model has already been proven time and time again.

The franchise is the combination of the Strickland family's two previously existing, highly respected brands, River Street Sweets and Savannah's Candy

Kitchen, both known nationally and worldwide. The two retail store chains are comprised of more than 18 stores with joint revenues exceeding $35 million.

The Strickland family brought the praline to Savannah in 1973 when they opened their flagship candy store, now the city's oldest, on River Street. Savannah's Candy Kitchen, a separate but similar entity and the largest candy store in the South, soon followed, as well as more stores under both names. After operating the brands independently for more than two decades, the Stricklands combined them to create their landmark franchise opportunity.

River Street Sweets • Savannah's Candy Kitchen franchises
include a variety of handmade Southern sweets.

"One of the main reasons to buy into the River Street Sweets•Savannah's Candy Kitchen franchise is because of the business model. It's a highly successful one," explained founding franchisee Glen Willard, who opened the first franchise location in Pooler, Georgia, in 2015. "If franchisees follow the proven business model, they can, with reasonable certainty, hope to have the same success."

Franchisees can depend on built-in knowledge and training instead of feeling like they're on a test run, he explained.

117

"The existing business model — with the training, recipes, operations manual — is all at your fingertips," he said. "The support of the corporate franchisor is always just a phone call away when you need help."

In fact, Willard expanded his interest in the brand and opened a second franchise location in Key West, Florida, in 2017.

"I've been an entrepreneur for many years, and this particular franchise is one that truly stands out," he continued. "This is just the beginning. It's a great opportunity for other potential franchisees to get in on the ground level while there's still room in some of the more popular territories, markets not already taken, that are predicted to have the most success."

The key, Willard said, is that people already know the brand — and are hungry for it, literally.

"When you become a franchisee for River Street Sweets•Savannah's Candy Kitchen, you immediately become part of the family," he explained. "You become part of a successful, recognizable brand that people already know and are excited about. People already know who we are because of the quality of the products and their long-standing tradition."

The demand is certainly there. According to the National Confectioners Association, the U.S. population consumes more than seven billion pounds of candy a year, more than any other country on the planet.

"When we decided to franchise our business, it was because we knew that people around the country would love our delicious Southern candies," said Jennifer Strickland. "Through franchising we're able to expand our business and distribute our one-of-a-kind products with a network of dedicated franchisees who are in this business for the same reasons we are — because we love candy."

A More Detailed History

Oh, fudge. That's how it all began.

Back in the early 1970s, young Tim Strickland was at the Atlanta Gift Market trade show with his big sister, Jennifer, and their parents, Stan and Pam. The family was there, hoping to find some items for The Cotton Bale, their gift shop back home on historic River Street in Savannah.

Glen and Liane Willard, the first franchisees, operate locations in Pooler, Georgia, and Key West, Florida.

Tim, who could be quite insistent at the tender age of 11, stumbled upon a fudge pot and begged his parents to put it in the store. His dad finally agreed, and, a week later, on St. Patrick's Day, Jennifer and Stan made the first batch of chocolate mint fudge. The fudge sold extremely well — much better than the gifts in the store — so Stan and Pam decided to start working on some candy recipes at home.

With Jennifer and Tim as the eager taste testers, mom and dad experimented with several praline recipes on the kitchen stove using simple ingredients: cream, butter, sugar, and Georgia pecans. They found a recipe they all loved and Stan began making pralines in the store. Not yet knowing that the marble slab (purchased back then from a local gravestone supplier) should be buttered, Stan dipped the pralines onto it, only to have them crumble when he tried to pick them up with a spatula. He handed the pieces out as samples, and customers loved it, starting a tradition that continues today in every store.

The pralines were so popular that they soon replaced the other gifts, and River Street Sweets became a full-fledged candy store. Today, the World Famous Pralines® help generate more than $35 million in annual sales, making River

Street Sweets•Savannah's Candy Kitchen the leading supplier of pralines on the planet.

The oldest candy store in Savannah, River Street Sweets is still family owned and operated by siblings Jennifer and Tim. Just down the street, their father, Stan "The Candy Man," heads up Savannah's Candy Kitchen, the largest candy store in the South since 1991.

Since then, the Stricklands have logged a combined 100 years of candy-making experience and made the South synonymous with Southern sweets known worldwide. The business has grown far beyond Savannah, with locations in Charleston and Myrtle Beach, South Carolina, as well as Atlanta, Nashville, and many more. Business then expanded into wholesale and mail order, with an extensive gift line of candies shipped countrywide throughout the year. The holidays are the busiest time for the stores. In fact, River Street Sweets•Savannah's Candy Kitchen is the United Parcel Service's biggest shipper in Savannah.

Today, guests continue to revel in the nostalgic experience of watching candymakers dip pralines, stretch peanut brittle, stir glazed pecans in huge copper kettles, and seeing the flagship store's 100-year-old saltwater taffy machine in action.

An Amazing Partnership

In 2014, the Strickland family combined their efforts to offer the best of both candy companies under the unified River Street Sweets•Savannah's Candy Kitchen brand. By doing so, they are now actively sharing their candy-making traditions by offering franchise opportunities around the country.

Besides actually being made in the stores, the candy and other sweets are also produced in and shipped from a 75,000-square-foot factory in Savannah that is FDA certified at the highest level available for wholesale facilities. The facility includes corporate offices, mail order headquarters, a commercial bakery, two candy-making kitchens, and a 4,000-square-foot chocolate production room. Corporate offices are also located above the original River Street Sweets location on River Street, where it all began.

Today, franchisees continue the tradition of hand-dipping pralines and giving out samples.

"As a franchisee, one of the things I like the most about operating our stores is the wonderful interaction we get to experience with customers," said Willard, who has recently been watching guests gobble up praline samples at his second franchise in Key West. "There's nothing like handing a guest a fresh, warm praline sample. There's a delayed response and then you know what's coming. They smile and say something like, 'Oh my gosh – that's just the best thing I've ever tasted!'"

The World Famous Pralines® are made fresh daily.

Loggerheads® and Giving Back

A gooey concoction of rich chocolate, creamy caramel, and crunchy pecan pieces are called by several other names, including Turtles® and Bear Claws®. River Street Sweets•Savannah's Candy Kitchen named theirs Loggerheads® in honor of local Savannah sea turtles.

In fact, they partnered with The Caretta Research Project for Loggerhead Sea Turtles, which is devoted to the conservation and protection of these beautiful,

121

threatened creatures. Each time they hold a grand opening ceremony for a new River Street Sweets•Savannah's Candy Kitchen franchise store, the Stricklands plan to donate all proceeds from loggerhead candy sales that day to Caretta.

The company also gives to various local and international organizations, including Senior Citizens, Inc., to help senior citizens in need, and Kids Cafe, to assist disadvantaged youth.

"Giving back has always been important to us," Jennifer Strickland said.

Other Sweet Favorites: Pecans and Saltwater Taffy

Eaten by themselves or as an added garnish to entrees, salads, and other desserts, River Street Sweets•Savannah's Candy Kitchen pecans are always savored. In fact, the Stricklands purchase over one million halves of Georgia pecans each year for the company's recipes.

In a show that never gets old, guests in Savannah's flagship locations always love watching candy artisans in action as they heat up the secret candy glaze recipe in shiny copper kettles. After the pecans are added, the mixture is stirred gently until it reaches 280 degrees. The candy artisans carefully pour the mixture onto marble slabs, and then painstakingly separate each glazed pecan from the other, one-by-one.

In addition to glazed pecans, they also make praline pecans, chocolate pecans, cinnamon pecans, and Chocolate Southern Charms: glazed pecans double-dipped in caramel and covered in creamy milk chocolate.

Saltwater taffy, all twenty-four flavors of it, is another favorite. At the flagship and in select locations, guests love to watch as the candy chefs pull the taffy on antique machines that are over one hundred and fifty years old. River Street's antique taffy machine was featured in the HBO series Boardwalk Empire.

A Growing Household Name

The Stricklands, who are busy finding new locations for franchises, constantly have people begging them to open stores, whether in the northern, southern, eastern or western United States and around the world.

"After many years of opening and operating our own stores in various locations, we knew that our expansion goals would only be met through engaging motivated and enthusiastic people to help grow our brand," said Jennifer Strickland. "By opening a number of corporate locations before franchising, we were able to hone in on exactly what to look for in future franchisees — people with outgoing, upbeat personalities looking for an exciting, time-tested business to run with tremendous growth potential."

She is particularly proud of Willard as the founding franchisee.

"We are so proud of the Willard family for going well beyond expectations," she said. "Glen surpassed his five-year business goal in his first year alone. That's incredible."

In the fall of 2017, another franchise opened in Lancaster, Pennsylvania. Stores expected to open in 2018 include New York City, Orlando, Florida, and several cities in Texas.

"This is a really exciting time," she continued.

A Sweet Payoff

The plan appears to be working. In addition to dozens of previous accolades for their initial brands, the combined franchise brand was recognized in 2017 as one of *Entrepreneur* magazine's Top New Franchises. In 2016, CNBC named it one of 11 Hot Franchises for summer. The franchise was also recently featured in *Forbes*, *Southern Living*, *Candy Industry*, and *Franchise Times* magazines. In 2017, Jennifer and Tim were named by *South* magazine as some of the South's greatest bosses.

During the next five years, the Stricklands anticipate opening at least 25 more franchises.

"We see the future being bigger than where we are today," said Jennifer Strickland. "We're really excited about taking our strong regional brand and making it national."

More Information

To learn how you can be like a kid in your own candy store by owning your own franchise, contact River Street Sweets•Savannah's Candy Kitchen! Call 888-842-9037, email info@riverstreetcandyfranchise.com, or visit www.riverstreetcandyfranchise.com.

123

A re you passionate about changing peoples' lives and making a difference in the world? If so, you may be a perfect fit for LINK Staffing.

Bill and Karen Pitts founded this business in 1980 and started franchising in 1994. Today they operate thirty-seven franchise offices, and they're looking to add more.

One of the amazing aspects of LINK Staffing is the company's reputation within the staffing industry, and that begins with the founders. The Pitts were founding members of the Texas Association of Staffing, and Karen served as chairman of the American Staffing Association and was inducted into the Leadership Hall of Fame. Daughter Michelle Bearden, who works in the franchise, also served on the board of the Texas Association of Staffing.

LINK Staffing offers these benefits to franchisees:

- Core values that guide the decisions made by the franchisor.
- The most thorough screening process in the industrial staffing and clerical staffing agencies segment.
- Commitment to continually improving the brand's technology to increase efficiency and to support client needs.
- A family environment that binds the corporate staff with franchisees.
- Commitment to finding talent for particularly hard-to-fill positions.

- Commitment to a sustainable system that will reduce labor costs and turnover, provide quality, flexible staffing solutions, and employ experienced people who are dedicated to meet and exceed clients' expectations.

Integrity is a huge part of any reputation, which helps explain why some franchisees have been with LINK Staffing for more than twenty years. It also helps explain how LINK Staffing is a dynamic and growing franchise opportunity. This may be the business for you – read the next chapter to learn more!

— Dr. John P. Hayes

LINK Staffing Franchisees Make a Difference in People's Lives

L anding a new job is something to celebrate. Imagine watching that joyous occasion unfold over and over each day at work as you and your staffing team fill countless job openings.

Kerry Simon of Baton Rouge, Louisiana, has been living that happy scenario for 21 years as a LINK Staffing franchise owner.

"If you like helping people, it's so rewarding," Simon says.

The staffing industry connects great people with thriving companies, and that's how LINK Staffing franchisees make a difference in people's lives and their communities.

"The majority of my clients are not just clients anymore. A lot of them have become friends," Simon continues. "You have to build a good rapport with them, and you have to be honest."

Specializing in Repeat Customers

That honesty, along with mutual respect, has won Simon not only genuine connections throughout the community but repeat clients as well.

As those placed employees move up through the ranks at work, they remember LINK Staffing when they are in the position to fill job openings.

Simon recalls a worker he placed at an apartment complex who returned years later, saying, "I remember you putting me to work. Now, I'm looking for you to help me out." Because of her great experience with LINK Staffing 10 years before, she returned to Simon's firm. Those personal triumphs are just a part of why Simon loves being a LINK Staffing franchisee.

"It's getting to the point that you go somewhere and you know people," he says. "The greatest advertising is word of mouth. If you do a good job, you get referrals. When someone walks in the door, I tell my employees, 'You treat somebody with respect. When they get in the position to hire people, they call us.'
"

126

Franchisee Pat Vasquez at renewal signing and planning for a second office expansion.

In Lewisville, Texas, franchisee Pat Vasquez is so enthusiastic about her LINK Staffing franchise and the success she has enjoyed that she's preparing to open a second office in Plano, a nearby suburb, next year. She says that being able to make someone's life better through job placement and possible advancement is what makes going to work every day a happy responsibility. It's not just a job; it's a passion.

Vasquez relishes "when candidates come in and we place them to work and they're very excited about working and being able to feed their families," she says.

One of the Fastest-growing B2B Industries

It's no secret that the world of work has changed. Under constant pressure to maximize efficiencies, business leaders turn to staffing firms to provide temporary workers during peak seasons when they need to flex up and down quickly. Direct hire, special projects, and vacancies are among other reasons companies partner with staffing firms.

As a result, staffing has grown into a $150 billion industry. According to the American Staffing Association, an average of 3.21 million temporary workers were placed in open positions each week in 2016.

In Vasquez's Texas office, more than 256 people were placed last year, generating over $5 million in revenues.

"The money potential is uncapped," Vasquez says. "The more positions we fill, the more money we make."

Candidate preferences have changed, too. Some, particularly younger candidates, prefer the flexibility of temporary and contract employment (often referred to the gig economy). Work-life balance, adjustable schedules, a variety of work experiences, new skill sets, and a bridge to full-time employment are some of the benefits of working with a staffing firm.

"I am passionate about serving my community. Owning a LINK franchise affords me the opportunity to do so by helping clients achieve business goals and providing meaningful work to our employees," says Amy Pope-Wells, a Jacksonville, Florida franchisee.

Anthony Carnevale says one of the great things about being a LINK franchisee is the exceptional support structure.

Support From the Home Office

LINK Staffing is a family-owned organization. That's why LINK is proud to live by an important set of principles: trustworthy, flexible, dependable, and ethical. And this supportive family culture extends to its franchisees who can count on LINK Staffing's support in both good times and bad.

"While we are expanding into new areas and reinventing ourselves to be a modern and nimble company poised to support that rapid expansion, we are staying true to the things that made LINK great," explains LINK President, Marc Rosenow.

When Baton Rouge, Louisiana, experienced a "500-year flood" in 2016, franchisee Simon found his office under three feet of water. Not only did they lose their computers and office furniture, but the staffing firm's essential paperwork was a total wash.

"When you lose your office and your employees lose their houses, it's devastating," he says.

While Simon and his staff regrouped in their personal lives, LINK Staffing's corporate office sent backup to run his office for two weeks, or as Simon calls them, "a big team in my back pocket to help me out so I could get back on my feet."

For Simon, LINK's VP of Franchise Operations, Michelle Bearden, was just a phone call away. A team was dispatched immediately from Houston headquarters.

"If it hadn't been for that, I wouldn't be in business today," Simon says. "It really made me appreciate the franchise. Sometimes you have to go through something like that to realize what you really have. I work well with them and they work well with me. I've been blessed."

Beyond corporate support, LINK also leads the staffing franchising field through competitive fees, larger territories, financial incentives, and industry-leading support and training.

- Financial Support: LINK offers low entrance fees, payroll funding for temporary workers, back-office management, and performance bonuses so franchisees can focus on building successful businesses rather than time-intensive administrative tasks.

- Larger Territories: In addition to larger territories, LINK offers longer franchise terms and more location possibilities to franchisees than other staffing franchisors.

- Marketing Support: The LINK Genius Award-winning Marketing department makes promotion easy for franchisees with lead-generating websites, brand management, video production, email and print templates, and graphic design assistance.
- Support Manager: All LINK franchisees are assigned a franchise support manager for guidance on day-to-day issues, best practice sharing, and advice on growth strategies and succession plans.

"As a new franchisee, one of the great things about being a LINK franchise owner is the support structure they have," says franchisee Anthony Carnevale. "Working with the different support departments added value to get us up to speed quickly and got us where we are today."

From its headquarters in Houston, LINK has produced a variety of proprietary programs for franchisees, clients and employees.

Differentiated Staffing Solutions

Demonstrating uniqueness in the staffing industry is a challenge, but after almost four decades, LINK Staffing has developed some amazing proprietary programs that resonate with both clients and employees.

- For clients: LINK provides flexible staffing solutions, candidate cultural fit matching, and a robust candidate assessment process. The LINK 9-Step Employee Selection System^{SM} furnishes reliable, dependable talent. LINK's 360 Safe Environment^{SM} Program administered by OSHA-certified professionals protects both clients and employees.

- For employees: LINK provides access to great jobs, great companies, and great assignments. Employees enjoy daily and weekly pay options, robust benefits, training opportunities, and employment options.

"We have a really good process that we go through, and it works," says Simon, who recalls how a previous staffing firm he worked for didn't require that prospective employees go through a drug screening. That approach created all sorts of issues. He was able to compare the vastly different results when he started working for LINK Staffing.

Franchisees also can't say enough about how LINK's staffing protocol is the best in the industry. Both Simon and Vasquez, who previously worked for other staffing firms, have seen firsthand how LINK's approach delivers the best employees to their clients.

Vasquez touts LINK's unique on-boarding process for employees, which helps find the right fit for the candidate and assures a successful fit for the company.

"We spend more time with the candidate when they come in than any other company I've worked for, as far as screening and making sure we have the right candidate for the right job. And we have the tools to screen in or screen out," she says. "The other agencies I worked for, they'd say, 'You're hired. Start tomorrow.'"

That proven, thorough process also means a positive work environment for Vasquez and her own employees. Because they believe in what they're doing and see firsthand amazingly positive results every day, there's no reason to look elsewhere for work. Around Vasquez's office, it's not unusual for her employees to be on the receiving end of bonuses and other perks.

"The retention rate is really high in our office. Attrition is low. That's huge," she says. "I share the love and give my employees bonuses, and we do team building and other events at least once a quarter. We have a bunch of little perks here."

Honoring Veterans and Diversity

LINK Staffing believes that diversity enriches the organization, and they strive to create an atmosphere where everyone feels valued and empowered to perform at peak levels. LINK is a member of DiversityFran through the International Franchise Association and over 25 percent of LINK franchise offices are minority-owned.

Military training and discipline are also considered valuable assets for a franchisee. Thirteen percent of LINK franchises are owned by military veterans.

"I served 11 years in the Marines, Staff Sgt. E-6. The last part of my service years were spent on recruiting duty. I feel that helped me transition well into staffing," says Barry Paradis, who has built the Charlotte, North Carolina, franchise into one of LINK's largest and most successful franchises with his wife, Mary.

LINK encourages additional franchise ownership and veteran hiring through several veteran-focused incentives:

- veterans wishing to open a LINK franchise receive special discounts, such as a reduced franchise fee;
- LINK is a member of the International Franchise Association's VetFran program;
- the LINKCorps™ staffing program helps vets find meaningful employment.

"After serving in the U.S. Navy as a Lieutenant, I spent 7 years in the corporate world before deciding to franchise," says franchisee James Merchant. "We opened our first LINK franchise in Tampa, Florida, in 1997, and today my wife and I own and operate three LINK franchise offices and one onsite."

Diversity is important at LINK and the management team strives to create an atmosphere where everyone feels valued and empowered to perform at peak levels.

40 Years of Amazing Success

At LINK, franchisees have access to a proven business model that has been fine-tuned based on nearly 40 years of experience. Founded in 1980 by Bill and Karen Pitts, LINK Staffing provides direct-hire, temp-to-hire, and temporary/contract employment services. LINK employs nearly 20,000 employees per year—or more than a half million total since its founding.

"We started our business focused on quality in the light industrial staffing space and operate as a boutique player committed to delivering superior service to employees and clients alike," says Bill Pitts, who serves as co-CEO with Karen.

In 1994, LINK began offering franchise opportunities to motivated entrepreneurs. Today, LINK Staffing has more than 40 locations nationwide, with more than 25 percent of LINK offices generating gross revenues in excess of $5 million per year.

"We enjoy spending time with the franchisees in our LINK family," says Karen. "Together we built an amazing company."

And it's not just the founders who consider it an amazing company. LINK Staffing is one of the most recognized and awarded staffing brands in America. Among the awards LINK received in 2017 are *Entrepreneur* magazine's Top 500 Franchises, Franchise Times 200+, American Staffing Association Genius Awards, Best of Staffing, and Best Places to Work. Other awards won by LINK Staffing include:

- Two Genius Awards from the American Staffing Association in the Social Media Campaign and Mobile Application categories, 2017
- *Entrepreneur* Franchise 500 list of the top-ranked Franchise Opportunities, 2017
- *Franchise Times* Top 200+ Franchises, 2016
- Inavero's Best Talent Service Staffing Agencies, 2016
- *Houston Business Journal* Best Places to Work, medium-sized companies, 2015-2017
- 2014 Staffing Industry Analysts Diversity Staffing Firm, 2014
- Inc. 5000 list of the 5000 Fastest Growing Private Companies, 2013

In addition, Karen Pitts has been inducted into the National Staffing Association's Hall of Fame to honor her extraordinary accomplishments in the industry.

More Information

If you're a motivated individual who enjoys variety and find fulfillment in helping others find gainful employment, LINK Staffing is a proven, unique and award-winning franchise opportunity. More information is available at 713-784-4400, ext. 9, or by contacting LINK via email at franchising@linkstaffing.com.

FULLY PROMOTED
Branded Products & Marketing Services

Most small businesses underperform.

That's just my opinion, I have no statistical data to prove it, but my opinion is based on a lifetime of experiences as a business adviser, coach, and franchisor.

I'm also of the opinion that most small businesses underperform because they are owned and operated by "technicians" and not by savvy business builders. We can thank Michael Gerber, author of *The E-Myth*, for explaining that technicians own businesses. Technicians are "busy, busy, busy, doing, doing, doing," says Gerber. They work "in" their businesses instead of "on" their businesses where they could get more favorable results.

Most small-business owners, especially technicians, need help to understand how to build their business without personally taking on more responsibility.

Yes, of course, we've always had consultants to advise small-business owners, but technicians, unfortunately, are too busy for consultations, or they don't see the point of it, or (more likely) they can't afford it. They'd rather suffer through the trials and tribulations of operating a marginal business than pay for advice.

That environment has created an opportunity for a new franchise! And it's called Fully Promoted.

For years, small-business owners have known Fully Promoted by its original name: EmbroidMe. Early on, Fully Promoted specialized in embroidered products for businesses, and customers (including many technicians!) loved the products and trusted the brand that provided the products.

Through the years, the EmbroidMe network, including franchisor United Franchise Group and many franchisees, realized that customers were asking for more than just embroidered products. Customers were asking for help! They needed help to expand and build their businesses. And they wanted to buy that help from a source they could trust.

In 2017, EmbroidMe changed its name to Fully Promoted and added numerous key services for small-business owners and managers. You'll get the full story in the next chapter. After reading it, you may want to join the Fully Promoted franchise network.

Are you a technician? Not to worry. Fully Promoted can help you build a prosperous and satisfying business!

— Dr. John P. Hayes

Fully Promoted: Promotional Marketing and Much, Much More

One afternoon, while working in his Signarama shop, Ray Titus answered a phone call from a college friend who owned a small business in New York that sold embroidered uniforms. The friend wanted to pick Ray's brain about expanding the business.

That conversation in 2000 led to Fully Promoted (formerly known as EmbroidMe) opening its doors right next to Signarama in North Palm Beach, Florida.

Since then, Fully Promoted has seen its share of changes. The company evolved from logos and embroidery to a full-service promotional marketing consulting company, specializing in marketing programs that meet businesses on their level and at their budget. To keep up with the broadening scope of the products and services that Fully Promoted franchisees provide to their customers, the brand recently underwent a complete refresh, including the name change.

Introducing: Fully Promoted

The name change was announced to more than two hundred franchisees at a brand conference in Las Vegas in early 2017. EmbroidMe would become Fully Promoted.

"The name change was extremely well thought out," explains Brand President Joe Loch. "We combined the expertise of our experienced brand experts at United Franchise Group (UFG) with that of an outside agency and with the expertise of our franchisees, who were acutely aware that their clients wanted a much broader range of services. But with the name EmbroidMe, most customers did not realize that we were so much more!"

In the $50 billion global promotional marketing industry, it takes a lot to come out on top, and Fully Promoted is proud to sit right in that sweet spot. For entrepreneurs who want to make an impact through customized marketing solutions, there is no better opportunity than Fully Promoted.

Promotional products have a far greater reach and impact than people might think. Consider the following:

- Eighty-three percent of customers say they enjoy receiving a promotional product with an advertising message.
- After receiving a promotional product, eighty-five percent of consumers say they end up doing business with the company.
- Fifty-eight percent of consumers keep a promotional product for up to four years.
- Eighty-nine percent of consumers can recall the advertiser on a promotional product that they received in the past two years.
- A promotional product increases the effectiveness of other media by forty-four percent.

Consistently ranked among *Entrepreneur* magazine's "Top Franchises to Own," Fully Promoted (ranked as EmbroidMe through January 2017) has a proven track record of success. In fact, for multiple years, Fully Promoted has ranked #1 in its category in "The Entrepreneur 500," an esteemed ranking of franchise systems based on factors such as financial strength, stability, and growth rate.

Adding to the services that EmbroidMe franchisees were already offering to their customer base, Fully Promoted now includes online marketing services, lead generation, and complete campaign management for a variety of marketing services. The expansion provides a comprehensive customer experience that attracts new customers. The possibilities are endless.

"We expect great things and are excited for the future of this newly innovated brand," says Ray Titus, founder and CEO of UFG. "It's one of the things I feel we do best here. We evolve our brands and stay relevant to the needs of our customers."

Fully Promoted franchisees offer an ever-expanding range of marketing and promotional services.

No Industry Experience Needed

As a Fully Promoted franchisee, you have the opportunity to develop repeat business relationships with volume-based clients. Promotional products are typically purchased in bulk quantities. This helps to keep costs down, while maintaining a high-perceived value for the customer. Coupled with online purchasing capabilities, this streamlines the ordering process and allows for minimal overhead. Higher sales and lower costs increase maximum earning potential for Fully Promoted franchisees.

No industry experience is required for Fully Promoted franchisees, although a keen business sense and some basic marketing knowledge helps franchisees succeed in this industry.

Edgar Gomez is a good example of a franchisee who joined Fully Promoted as a veteran of another industry: oil and gas. With more than twenty years of experience in that field, Gomez knew that all of the knowledge he collected along the way would serve him well in an entirely new endeavor.

"During the years that I had worked in the oil and gas industry," he explained, "I had a great deal of success in many challenging situations, so I felt prepared to become a small-business owner. Whether it's managing personnel or working under pressure to serve a client, I'm looking forward to building a successful business. Even though I'm only fifty, I believe Fully Promoted will provide a foundation for my eventual retirement."

Since there's an ongoing need for companies to spread the word, the promotional products industry can count on repeat business going forward.

According to IBISWorld, which publishes market research, the promotional products industry is estimated at more than $20 billion in the U.S. alone. This is due in large part to the desire for businesses and industries to extend the reach of their brand, be it through custom embroidery, promotional products, or personalized gifts.

With such a diverse mix of goods and services, the Fully Promoted franchise model is virtually recession-proof. Products range from marketing material and trade-show equipment to apparel and team uniforms to lead generation and online marketing services. Demand for these types of products and services will persist through any foreseeable economic conditions. This gives new and prospective franchisees peace of mind as they embark on their new business venture.

"I chose Fully Promoted (then EmbroidMe) because I had a big connection with the community, and after a lot of research, I thought it was a perfect fit. The support that they offer, and easing into this business as opposed to the business I had before, was perfect for me," explained Angelo Bonvino of Nanuet, New York, a franchisee since 2004.

It's a Far-Reaching Industry

Every business benefits from marketing services and/or promotional materials. Offering a free product with a logo and contact information can have a lasting impact, which is applicable to almost any industry.

A few of the business categories that Fully Promoted franchisees currently support are:

- Restaurants
- Clubs and schools
- Medical companies
- Sports teams
- Professional services
- Automotive brands
- Private online stores

"The possibilities are truly endless, limited only by the franchisee's creativity and desire to build a business," says Joe Loch, brand leader.

E-commerce is a trillion-dollar industry and is growing at a double-digit rate every year. It only makes sense that a promotional products company would capitalize on such a market.

Statistically, companies that offer an online order option enjoy 7 percent higher sales than companies that do not. Fully Promoted has successfully established an online presence, allowing customers to purchase what they need without necessarily having to set foot in a brick-and-mortar location.

Critics may claim that online sales prevent the organization from being able to truly service its customers, ultimately prohibiting upselling. On the contrary, Fully Promoted franchisees see the benefit in offering built-in conveniences to their customers. A person or business that already knows what they want will appreciate the ease of ordering online. A business owner who understands exactly what he or she needs appreciates the opportunity to order online from Fully Promoted. Meanwhile, business owners who need guidance are pleased to know that a Fully Promoted resource center exists nearby. One channel does not cannibalize the other; rather, they work in tandem to reach even more customers.

Thanks to Fully Promoted's advanced technology, promotional products are now limited only by a customer's imagination.

An Umbrella of Services

Technology plays a vital role in the embroidery, promotional products, and marketing services industries – all of which are facilitated through Fully Promoted's umbrella of services.

"In the past," explains Loch, "there were limits to the types of products that could be emblazoned with a brand name or logo. Today, through advancements in computer software and machinery, promotional products are only limited by the customer's imagination. With the advent of 3D printing, for example, technology is changing the landscape for promotional products, and costs are no longer prohibitive."

Purchasing a Fully Promoted franchise is a turnkey investment, meaning all equipment, hardware, software, fixtures, and furnishings are included in the initial investment. UFG conducts extensive demographic research in the desired market area, then assists new franchisees with site selection, lease negotiation, and coordination of each store's build-out.

The Fully Promoted franchise fee is a flat amount – $49,500 – paid at the time of signing the franchise agreement. Fully Promoted's fee was developed based on several factors, including the right to use the Fully Promoted name and other brand-specific systems and operational advantages.

Franchisees need $50,000 working capital, which essentially means they have the funds to see the business through to profitability. UFG, and the Fully Promoted franchise system specifically, wants to ensure that a franchisee has the financial means to build the business during the initial launch period and until a profit can be realized.

As a Fully Promoted franchisee, you can expect to invest between $135,000 and $140,000 to get started. This amount varies depending on: location of the business, set-up and equipment needs, operational costs, insurance, and other expenses. Third-party financing is available to cover up to 70 percent of the total investment.

Fully Promoted franchisees pay 6 percent of their monthly gross sales as a royalty to UFG. The royalty helps underwrite costs relative to ongoing brand support, resources provided by the brand and UFG, and associated expenses that contribute to the company's overall growth. The fee also helps solidify Fully Promoted's reign as the world's leading promotional products franchise.

UFG and Fully Promoted wholeheartedly believe that with a sound business model and plan in place, franchisees will succeed. That's why the company puts the utmost importance on training and support.

"I had hired a new salesperson for my store and the UFG field rep spent the better part of the day with us, reviewing our goals and outlining the business model for my staff," explains Jeff Henges, a franchisee in Torrance, California. "The field rep even spent time on the road with our new hire to make marketing calls. I can't thank UFG and the field rep enough for the continued commitment to ensuring that we have the tools we need to achieve success."

Fully Promoted franchisees have the expertise and support of a seasoned brand behind them. Buying into a franchise at UFG also means buying into a network of fellow franchisees to lean on and collaborate with for the life of the business.

Fully Promoted franchisees have access to multiple support programs as well. Some of these include:

- Regional meetings & training sessions
- Regional support staff
- Owner conventions
- Technical support
- A dedicated toll-free number and online support

As part of the highly-successful UFG family of franchises,
Fully Promoted offers extensive training and support for its franchisees.

An Award-Winning Franchise

Fully Promoted is very proud to have been ranked #1 in its category on *Entrepreneur's* prestigious Franchise 500 list many times over the years. The brand also consistently ranks high in the "overall" category as well. In 2016, the company ranked #130 out of 500 and solidified its #1 in category yet again.

A few other brief highlights of Fully Promoted's industry-recognized accomplishments are:

- *Franchise Direct*
    - 2014: Franchise Direct Top 100 Global Franchises – Ranked #39
- *Promo Marketing*
    - 2016: Promo Marketing's Top 50 Distributors List – Ranked #15
    - 2015: Promo Marketing's Top 50 Distributors List – Ranked #15
    - 2014: Promo Marketing's Top 50 Distributors List – Ranked #14
    - 2013: Promo Marketing's Top 50 Distributors List – Ranked #13
- *Counselor* magazine
    - 2006 - 2015: Top 40 Distributor List – Ranked as high as #13!
    - 2006 - 2012: Counselor Power 50 Award – Ranked as high as #10!

144

– 2007: Counselor International Person of the Year – Ray Titus

• *Stitches* magazine

– 2010 – 2014: Power 75, recognized Ray Titus

In a training video about UFG's mentor program (where experienced franchisees mentor new franchisees), one of Fully Promoted's longest-running and successful franchisees, Robert Pouliot, told a class of new franchisees: "You develop friendships and relationships, and everybody truly looks out for each other when you become a franchisee."

He pointed out that there's a vested interest for each franchisee and UFG to work together and create a support system for each other.

"It increases the value of our brand," Pouliot continued. "So, if and whenever we are ready to sell our store, there will be value in it; there will be more knowledgeable stores. The reason our business grew so quickly is because we could simply call our mentors and say, 'Hey, where can I get this or that?' 'How do I do this or that for my customer?' We got into this without any industry-related experience, but when a customer stands in front of us, we can say with confidence, 'Sure, we can do that,' and know that with help from UFG and other franchisees, we'll be able to service that customer."

Pouliot summed it up best when he said, "My take is very simple. We have this pool of people that amongst them have many years of experience in this business. I'm just leveraging it."

More Information

Think you might want to leverage this franchise opportunity? Contact Fully Promoted for more information at https://fullypromotedfranchise.com or call 877-406-0028.

The franchisor of Jon Smith Subs wants to see "a line of customers out the front door who want to eat here and a line of people out the back who want to work here." That's been the experience in Jon Smith Subs' home market in West Palm Beach, Florida, and now that experience is moving across the state and onto the national scene.

The Jon Smith Subs story is a great example of how some franchises are born. Smith founded his business in Palm Beach County and attracted a faithful following. When he decided to expand the business, he thought about franchising, which led him to Andy Cagnetta, founder of Transworld Business Advisors (TBA), another Florida-based enterprise that had recently begun franchising worldwide. Smith thought he might take a similar path, but he didn't know anything about franchising.

Not too many years earlier, Cagnetta was not familiar with franchising, either. However, he partnered with Ray Titus, founder and CEO of United Franchise Group based in West Palm Beach, Florida, to launch TBA's franchise network. When Smith contacted Cagnetta and explained his aspirations, Cagnetta introduced him to Titus. Shortly thereafter, Jon Smith Subs became a franchise brand!

Under the leadership of United Franchise Group, Jon Smith Subs has sold franchises in major U.S. cities.

Lines are forming, including the line of people who want to buy a Jon Smith Subs territory! If this is your type of business, you'll enjoy the full story in the next chapter.

— Dr. John P. Hayes

Jon Smith Subs Takes a Fresh Approach to Restaurant Franchising

The "journey into freshness" began in 1988 when Jon Smith purchased two sub shops in West Palm Beach, Florida. He transformed the menu, pricing, and overall operations, and then attracted more customers. When Smith introduced a new prototype for the business, he generated even more revenue. Today, there are nearly a dozen Jon Smith Subs locations across Palm Beach County, Florida, and franchising opportunities are being "swallowed up" across Florida and the United States!

Today Jon Smith is all about great subs, but his journey to providing the best subs in the business has taken some interesting turns. While passionate about quality in the sandwich industry, he's also an avid motorcycle rider, pilots small planes, and he's been a horse trainer. He's won race car championships, formed his own band, and still had time to hone his business acumen in several other industries. In the past, Smith developed an ice cream concept, opened a restaurant, and owned swimwear stores.

Jon Smith Subs is positioned for rapid growth nationwide.

Taking a Business to New Heights

Hoping to take his sub business to new heights, Smith reached out to Transworld Business Advisors CEO Andy Cagnetta for advice about franchising. In turn, Cagnetta brought the concept to Ray Titus, founder and CEO of United Franchise Group (UFG), but Ray was initially hesitant to venture into the food industry. Smith's expertise and the reputation he had solidified for his brand during the previous two decades eventually persuaded Titus to entertain the idea, and thus began UFG's foray into great sandwiches and the fast-casual dining industry.

Once a franchise plan was in place, UFG began a thorough search to find a brand leader who could step Jon Smith Subs through the intricacies of franchising. Generally, brand leaders grow up in the UFG network, but in the case of fast-casual dining, UFG required someone with food experience. Eventually, Smith brought a fellow restaurateur to UFG as a potential candidate. Scott Stuck had grown up in the food industry the way Ray Titus grew up in franchising. In other words, the food industry is in Stuck's blood the way franchising is in Titus' blood!

As a youngster, Stuck worked with his father, who was a franchisee for Elias Brothers Big Boy Restaurants (think burgers and checkered tablecloths). In college he studied hospitality, and as his first "real job," he spent eight years with Brinker International (the company that owns Chili's and Maggiano's restaurants, among other franchise brands).

As a regional vice president for Miller's Ale House, Stuck expanded the local sports pub favorite to about twenty locations in south Florida. But then he also invested his own money as a franchisee of Einstein Bros. Bagels, bd's Mongolian Grill, and Charlie Graingers, all of which gave him a well-rounded perspective to lead Jon Smith's Subs.

Jon Smith Subs stands out in the $700 Billion+ restaurant industry.

A Recipe for Success

The National Restaurant Association continually updates key indicators and trends in the marketplace, noting that restaurant industry sales currently exceed $782.7 billion! However, with more than one million restaurants operating in the United States, a restaurateur needs a concept to stand out. Fortunately, Jon Smith Subs meets the demand.

Customers of Jon Smith Subs experience the "thrill of the grill," getting what they truly want to eat with a wide range of customized menu options, including piping hot, award-winning fries. In fact, Jon Smith Subs' French fries were voted #1 out of the top ten French fries in Palm Beach County in a reader's choice poll at PalmBeachPost.com.

Jon Smith Subs franchisees make a commitment to their customers to only purchase quality cuts of real sirloin steak and chicken, as well as sourcing farm-fresh vegetables. They also bake their sub rolls daily in onsite ovens. At Jon Smith Subs, food is never microwaved, never steamed, never pre-cooked or pre-heated. It's a difference that customers can see and taste.

And if there is any room left after finishing your delicious, overstuffed sub, many Jon Smith Subs locations also offer fresh-baked chocolate chip cookies. These come highly recommended by UFG corporate staff who serve as willing taste testers during training sessions!

Brand President Scott Stuck says his vision for the future of Jon Smith Subs "is to have a line of customers out the front door who want to eat here and a line of people out the back who want to work here."

UFG is dedicated to the success of each Jon Smith Subs franchisee and, therefore, has systems and people in place to provide world-class training, operations, and marketing support. Brand professionals provide comprehensive training, marketing launch expertise, and ongoing collaboration and assistance to help ensure that each location gets the attention it needs to get off the ground quickly and then grow successfully – which is a clear recipe for success!

More Information

The growth of Jon Smith Subs is well underway with deposits for franchises in Miami, Orlando, Atlanta, Dallas, Houston, and other major cities throughout the U.S. Would you like to know more about this franchise opportunity? If so, follow this link: https://jonsmithsubsfranchise.com or call 888-351-2980.

Amazing Franchise Tools

17 Steps to Successfully Buying a Franchise

Everything is possible with a system!

Outstanding achievements are the result of someone following a system. With the right systems, you can succeed at almost anything. What is it that you want? There's a system to help you get it.

You want to successfully buy a franchise? It won't surprise you, I don't think, to discover that there's a system for doing so. And here it is: "17 Steps to Successfully Buying a Franchise." If you follow these guidelines, you're taking all the right steps to explore franchising, to consider the pros and cons of franchising, and, if franchising makes sense for you, to ultimately find a franchise opportunity worthy of your investment.

Even though I cannot guarantee your success as a franchisee—no one can because there are so many variables at play—if you complete these seventeen steps, you can eventually sign your name to a franchise agreement with the confidence that you've done everything possible to ensure your own success as a franchisee. Of course, you must follow the system and complete each step with integrity.

Based on that understanding, here are the 17 steps to successfully buying a franchise:

1.) Educate Yourself

As you prepare to buy a franchise, spend time reading (or viewing informational videos) to make sure you understand what franchising is all about. You can also get good information at franchise conferences and through franchise advisers. One way or another, get familiar with the fundamentals of franchising.

Questions you should ask:

- Why is franchising so successful?
- What are the main reasons for franchise failure?
- How can I be sure that a franchisor is legitimate?

2.) Why Franchising Exists

Of all the points that you need to understand about franchising, the most important may be this: Franchising is a system of distribution. Franchising is a means for marketing and selling products and services. Don't get caught up in any of the hype about franchising. Yes, of course, it's a way for you to own your own business, and it may be the safest way to do so, and it may be your ticket to financial independence, but do not overlook the fundamental purpose of franchising: It's to sell stuff!

Questions you should ask:

- Am I excited about distributing the franchisor's products and services?
- Do I see myself operating this system for five, ten, or more years
- How can I be sure that the franchisor's system will work in my territory?

3.) Are You a Good Fit for Franchising?

Be absolutely sure that franchising makes sense for you. Franchisors are not interested in selling franchises to the wrong prospects or investors. You should be equally as protective of yourself. Ask the question: Is franchising for me? Keep in mind that it's not for everyone. If it's not for you, don't force it. Read the chapter, "Match Your Personality to the Appropriate Franchise Opportunities" and complete the free DiSC assessment, www.howtobuyafranchise.com/disc.

Questions you should ask:

- What qualifies me to be a franchisee?
- Why do I want to be a franchisee?
- What type of franchise will make the most sense for me?

4.) Know Your Role as a Franchisee

Understand that the franchisor creates the system and the franchisees follow the system. Good franchisors know what needs to be done day to day, month to month, to succeed in the business. And that's what they'll expect you to do. Everything you're required to do is part of the system…so you must be willing to follow it, even if you don't always agree with it. Otherwise the franchisor can take away your franchise. The franchise agreement mandates that you follow the franchisor's system.

Questions you should ask:

- How can I learn more about the franchisor's system?
- What aspects of the system may or may not be of interest to me?
- Do existing franchisees endorse the franchisor's system?

5.) You're Buying a License

By legal definition, a franchise is a license. A franchisor licenses a franchisee to operate a specific business in a specific manner at a specific location (or in a specific region) for a specific period of time. The license can be renewed and either party also can terminate it. Be sure you understand those details before you invest.

Furthermore, the franchisor retains ownership of (almost) everything! The franchisor's intellectual property, training materials, marketing methodologies, sales processes, possibly even phone numbers and clients, always remain the property of the franchisor, and not the franchisee. These details will be explained in the Franchise Disclosure Document.

Questions you should ask:

- What are the specific terms of the franchise agreement?
- Do I get a protected territory? (You may not want a protected territory and you do not necessarily need one, depending on the franchise.)
- What if I decide I want to sell the franchise; how do I do that?

6.) The Franchise Work Environment

Think about the franchise work environment. Most franchisors require franchisees to be owners/operators. In other words, you can't be an absentee owner. Some franchisors expect franchisees to work from home, or a small office. Other franchisors require franchisees to work from a retail shop at a strip center or a mall. Other franchisors require franchisees to work from a van or another type of vehicle. In some cases, franchisees work alone; in other cases, franchisees manage employees. Once you know which work environment makes sense for you, pursue franchise opportunities that support your preferences.

Questions you should ask:

- Do I want to manage people?
- Am I comfortable working alone, from my home or a small office
- If I prefer one work environment but the franchise companies of my choice require a different work environment, can I adjust?

7.) Did You Know They Franchised That?

There are at least seventy-five primary industries that use franchising as their method of distribution. When people explore franchising, they're often surprised by the industries that use franchising as a methodology and by the vast array of franchise opportunities available. Some realize, for the first time, that franchising isn't just fast food! By reading this book, you'll discover franchises that provide cleaning, restoration, training, painting, recruitment, business services, and pet services, to name just several. What's important is to find the industry and the opportunity—or opportunities—that make sense for you.

Questions you should ask:

- Which industries interest me the most?
- Which industries can I afford?
- Which industries provide me with the best opportunities?

8.) Look for the Right Opportunity

No one knows exactly how many franchise opportunities exist, but there are three thousand to four thousand opportunities in North America alone. Many of these opportunities are local or regional, and some of the companies are sold out, so they're not offering franchises except internationally. Some industries include a dozen or more franchise companies offering similar and competitive franchise

155

opportunities, while other industries may only include a handful of franchise opportunities.

Of course, these numbers are of little consequence considering that you're looking for just one franchise: The one that's best for you. You will find these opportunities by reading books and articles, attending expos, and by being observant: What's being franchised today that interests you?

Questions you should ask:

- How much money can I invest in a franchise? The answer may dictate the industries that you should explore.
- How do I want to spend the next five, ten, or more years of my life in business?
- When it comes to "selling stuff," what excites me?

9.) Information is Free; Ask for It!

When you find a company that interests you, ask for information. It's free, and it comes without any strings attached. Remember this: A U.S.-based franchisor must provide U.S. citizens with a disclosure document at least two weeks before selling a franchise. The clock doesn't begin to tick until you acknowledge receiving the disclosure document. I want to emphasize the document is free.

However, franchisors will not give you the disclosure document until they've had an opportunity to speak with you and know that you are qualified to invest in their business. You can expect the franchisor (via online entry or an interview with a representative) to ask you for your personal information, including your email address, phone number, the time frame in which you plan to buy a franchise, and an estimate of how much money you intend to invest in a business. You also may be asked for specific financial information. By the way, it's a mistake to provide misleading information—once you're found out, do you think the franchisor will trust you?

Questions you should ask:

- Are you planning to open franchises in my territory of choice?
- How much is the investment in your franchise?
- What makes your franchise business unique and amazing?

10.) Carefully Read the Information

Invest time to carefully read the preliminary information provided by the franchisor. Make sure you not only can see yourself as a franchisee in this concept, but that you at least preliminarily understand what you'll be expected to do as a franchisee. The information the franchisor provides may not be specific, but the information in the franchisor's disclosure document must be specific. If you like the initial information you get from a franchisor, then it's time to ask for the disclosure document.

Questions you should ask:

- If I were to invest in this franchise, what else would I need to know?
- Is this a business that makes sense for my location, or territory?
- Where's this business headed in the next five to ten years?

11.) Attend the Franchisor's Discovery Day

Visit the franchisor. Almost every franchisor sponsors a Discovery Day. It might be called by another name—Decision Day, Information Day, etc. This is your chance to visit the franchisor's headquarters, meet company representatives, possibly even franchisees, and learn more about the franchise opportunity by listening to a variety of presentations and asking questions. The franchisor may also include a tour of the headquarters to show you the training center, the marketing department, franchise support, etc.

Franchisors do not charge a fee for Discovery Days, but it's likely you'll be expected to provide your own transportation and lodging. If you're married, the franchisor may want your spouse to attend, too.

Don't hesitate to ask the franchisor to pay for your expenses, or to share your expenses. Depending on how eager the franchisor is to sell a franchise, you may get a free trip. But even if you have to shell out some money for this experience, it's worth it. What's several hundred dollars when you're investing several thousand if not hundreds of thousands?

Questions you should ask:

- How is this business unique and amazing?
- How does this business compare to similar franchises?
- What's the future for this industry, and this franchise in particular?

12.) Get Disclosed

Ask the franchisor for the Franchise Disclosure Document (FDD) and prepare to read it thoroughly—a couple of times. This document is written in clear English so it's fairly easy to comprehend. However, you'll probably want a franchise attorney to review the document with you.

Once the franchisor knows that you're a "serious" candidate to buy a franchise, by law the franchisor must "disclose" you before continuing to talk to you about the franchise opportunity. This is a very serious matter and franchisors are careful not to violate it.

Disclosure does not obligate you in any way! It's a formality that must occur before you can buy a franchise. In fact, until you're disclosed, you cannot legally pay the franchisor any money. The franchisor must disclose you at least 14 days prior to you buying the franchise.

Just remember: You're not obligated until you sign the franchise agreement. The FDD is one document; the franchise agreement another. However, the franchise agreement mirrors the FDD.

Questions you should ask:

- How long has this franchise been in business; who owns it; how are the franchise company's executives qualified to be in their positions?
- How much training and support will I receive? Does it cost extra money?
- How often (if ever) have franchisees sued the franchisor, and why?

13.) Go to Work for a Franchisee

One of the most important steps you can take before buying a franchise is to talk to existing franchisees. Call them, visit them, and spend time with them. The FDD includes a list of existing and former franchisees—use that list; it's one of the most important tools for franchise exploration.

Existing franchisees will talk to you by phone, or if they're in close proximity to you, they may invite you for a personal meeting. Some franchisees may not be willing to talk to you at all, but most franchisees remember what it was like when they were exploring franchise opportunities and they're willing to help you because someone once helped them. Franchisees also realize that it's important for their franchise networks to expand—it gives them greater visibility in the marketplace (more franchisees means more money in the national advertising fund), and greater clout when negotiating with suppliers.

Here's an idea that you will find extremely helpful: Go to work for an existing franchisee. Offer to work weekends, or part time, for a month or more to experience the franchise operation. This is a practical way for you to discover your interest in a specific business. Many franchisors will require that you at least meet with an existing franchisee to discuss your prospects for joining the franchise network.

"Are franchisees getting paid to tell me good things so that I'll buy the franchise?" If they are, the information will be revealed in the FDD, or the franchisor is violating federal laws in the U.S. Generally, franchisors do not pay franchisees for speaking to prospective franchisees. However, franchisors sometimes sponsor competitions, i.e., the franchisee who helps sell the most franchises in a year receives $10,000! But that information also must be disclosed in the FDD.

Questions you should ask:

- Would you buy this same franchise again?
- What are the franchisor's greatest strengths...weaknesses?
- How much money can I expect to earn after a year as a franchisee? After three years?

14.) Decide if You Can Afford the Investment

Study Item 7 of the franchisor's FDD to understand your financial commitment when you buy this franchise. Federal law requires U.S. franchisors to clearly disclose financial information in the FDD. Item 7, Estimated Initial Investment, presents each financial commitment in a chart that shows you when the money is due to be paid, to whom it must be paid (i.e., the franchisor, a media company, a landlord, or a supplier), and whether or not the money is refundable. This is the best way to see the required financial commitment at a glance.

Keep in mind that the franchisor must include every financial requirement in Item 7, which eliminates surprises. "Oh, we didn't tell you that you must pay $5,000 for training?" That sort of thing shouldn't happen anymore in franchising.

Questions you should ask:

- Can I afford to invest this amount of money?
- Do existing franchisees say that the investment is reasonable?
- How does this financial commitment compare to investments in competitive opportunities?

15.) Understand the Ongoing Fees

Look at the ongoing royalty and advertising fee requirements, which are not part of Item 7. Most franchisors require franchisees to pay a percentage of gross sales as a royalty every month—the percentage may be as low as 5 percent and as high as 12 percent, and varies from company to company. The advertising fee is also a percentage of gross sales and may be in the range of 1 percent to 3 percent paid monthly.

Questions you should ask:

- Do the royalty and advertising fees seem reasonable?
- How does the franchisor spend the royalty dollars paid by franchisees?
- Is the national advertising fund effective for boosting retail sales?

16.) Get Help!

Consult with your professional advisers. You should spend the money to engage a franchise attorney and an accountant prior to signing a franchise agreement. There are many franchise attorneys at work in the U.S. and other countries; you can find them through a franchise association such as the International Franchise Association (www.franchise.org). You will likely pay $500 to $1,500 for the attorney's basic services, paying more to an attorney who does not specialize in franchise law—that's like asking your franchise attorney to handle a personal injury suit. If an attorney suggests he/she negotiate with the franchisor on your behalf, be very careful. Franchisors rarely negotiate and franchise attorneys know that. However, franchise attorneys also know areas in which a franchisor is likely to negotiate and may be helpful in that regard.

It's more difficult to find an accountant who is familiar with franchising and who understands franchising. Too often accountants are anti-franchising and they advise their clients to start businesses independently rather than to join a franchise network and pay fees. That's unfortunate because statistics demonstrate that in many industries franchises are more successful than independently owned businesses.

My best advice for finding a "franchise friendly" accountant is to find an accountant who is also a franchisee! In other words, the accountant's practice is part of a franchise network. Again, you can find these businesses through franchise associations or by asking franchisors and franchisees for referrals. A good accountant will be able to help you develop a business plan and assess your financial risk, as well as rewards. Accounting fees vary widely, but for basic services expect to pay $500 to $1,500. Keep in mind that you also may need an accountant after you become a franchisee to prepare your quarterly and annual statements.

Note that professional advisers are not supposed to make decisions for you. "Should I buy this franchise?" is a question that a good adviser will not answer. Advisers will point out the pros and cons; ultimately, you make the decisions.

Other possible advisers include franchise brokers and coaches. When you engage these advisers, make certain that you understand what's in it for them.

Brokers sell franchises for a living; they do not advise franchise prospects except as part of their mission to sell a franchise. Brokers generally do not charge fees to their clients because the franchisor pays them when they sell a franchise. There's nothing wrong with this arrangement, by the way, and franchisors who rely on brokers must reveal this information in the FDD.

Questions you should ask:

- How does this franchise opportunity compare to others you've reviewed?
- What are the problem areas that you see investing in this type of franchise?
- Based on my financial situation, is this a franchise I can afford?

17.) Make Your Final Decision

Take a deep breath, offer up any final prayers, and say "yes" to the franchisor of your choice. Go ahead; sign the franchise agreement. Congratulations, you're a franchisee! If you did your homework, and followed the recommendations offered to you in this book, you're on your way to stardom!

Questions you should ask:

- When does my training session begin?
- What three things must I be sure to do to succeed in this business
- What three things must I be sure not to do to succeed in this business?

When I'm buying a franchise, and when I coach my clients who are buying franchises, I use these 17 steps to success. Each step includes multiple tasks, and it's important to take the time to complete each step. If you have questions about how to complete these steps, or you need additional guidance, visit my website: HowtoBuyaFranchise.com and contact me.

How to Investigate Before You Invest in a Franchise

Adapted from Taking the Fear Out of Franchising published in 2017.

For as long as I can remember, the International Franchise Association (IFA) has advised consumers to *investigate before investing* in a franchise. It's great advice, responsible advice, and yet it's often ignored.

Too often, people invest in a franchise only to find out in a matter of months that they don't like the business or they can't succeed at the business or they don't want to operate the business, or any number of other *cant's* and *don'ts*.

"I didn't realize I'd have to spend so much time in the business" . . . "I can't handle all the turnover. I don't like working with young people. They don't want to work hard." . . . "I can't pay the royalty *and* make enough for myself." . . . "I really don't like my franchisor." . . . "I don't want to give up so much control to the franchisor."

These are among the most common complaints that I hear from people who buy franchises and then decide it was a poor decision.

"So what now?" I ask them. Of course, they come to me hoping that I'll have a solution for them and I do, but they won't like it.

It's too late to ask them, "Did you investigate before you invested?" They'll say, "Yes, of course," but upon further questioning they'll begin to realize they didn't do enough investigating. They didn't ask the pertinent questions. They didn't take the time to experience the franchise before investing in it. It makes no sense—*ever*—to invest hundreds of thousands of dollars in a business—or for that matter, as little as $10,000—and not do the necessary homework.

Maybe it's the word *necessary*. Some people apparently don't think franchise pre-investment homework is necessary, so they don't do it, or they don't do enough of it, or they don't know how to do it. And it's foolish to expect franchisors to insist on prospects doing the necessary homework. Yes, some franchisors do insist on it, but many, especially if they're eager to make a sale, don't. The law doesn't say they have to. After all, if you're in a position to buy a business, shouldn't you know that it's necessary to investigate thoroughly?

Some people will say they thought the franchise disclosure process protected them and so it wasn't necessary to give the franchise opportunity more than a cursory look. Others will say they thought it was enough to sit with their attorney to understand the franchise requirements and a "deep dive" into the nitty gritty of the business wasn't necessary.

But it is necessary! And yes, the disclosure process does indeed protect you, but mostly it protects you by requiring franchisors to provide pertinent information about the business. It can't do more than that. But *you* can. You can use the information the franchisor must provide to find out if you're a good fit for a specific business. That's where many people fail themselves. People who are actually a good fit for franchising often end up buying the wrong franchise! They buy a retail concept when they're a better fit for a service business, or they choose a food franchise but should have bought a business they could operate from home. And so on.

Unfortunately, when you don't do the necessary homework and you buy a franchise that's not a good fit, there's really not much you can do but sell the business and take your losses. It's not a popular solution, but do you have a better one? You can always try to change your mind about the franchisor, your employees, your customers, your location, your commitment, or with the hope of changing your mind about the business, but that's probably not a realistic solution. If you and the business are not a fit, it's not going to work. Get out of it. Better yet, don't ever put yourself in that position.

The IFA's advice: *Investigate before you invest* is the best way to protect yourself. Do it!

To help you, I've provided the following guidelines. Use these steps to complete the necessary homework, or the due diligence, that will lead you to make a good decision when you invest in a franchise.

Pay Attention to the Only Data That Matters

Due diligence is the process by which you "investigate" the franchise opportunity or opportunities that most interest you.

Unfortunately, many people fail Due Diligence 101. They either ignore it, they don't know how to collect the data, or they don't know how to analyze the data to arrive at reasonable conclusions.

You can do your own investigation, or you can hire someone to help you, although I don't recommend the latter because ultimately the decision to "buy" or "not to buy" a franchise rests with you.

Do you really want to invest your life savings in a business that someone else told you to buy?

Or not to buy?

Every year, even though it's been more than half a century, I still hear people say they're kicking themselves for not buying a McDonald's franchise when they had the opportunity. "If only I hadn't listened to my neighbor."

No Need to Investigate Franchising

Many experts, including consultants and advisers whom you might engage, formally or informally, will tell you that step one of your due diligence must be an investigation of franchising as a concept, or as an industry.

But I am telling you that's a waste of your time.

And here's why.

It's a Squishy Industry

No one knows for certain how many franchisor companies exist in America, or anywhere in the world, because franchisors are not required to register or to declare themselves as franchisors. Yes, every franchisor in the United States must file a disclosure document before selling a franchise, but no one's counting.

And you can be sure there are some businesses that sell franchises without filing a disclosure document, either on purpose or for lack of knowledge. These businesses may say they're selling "business opportunities," not franchises, but what they're actually doing is skirting onerous and costly franchise regulations, most likely to the detriment of the people who buy from them.

But since no one keeps track of the number of franchisor companies, the best guestimates say there are some three thousand to four thousand franchisors in North America. The number expands annually. The IFA says that new franchisor companies increase by about ten percent every year. Of course, since no one officially tracks franchise companies, no one knows how many franchisor companies fail or close their doors each year.

Are you getting the idea that franchising is a squishy industry?

Some specific data about franchises overall does exist. For example, the IFA reports that nearly three-fourths (73 percent) of franchisors support fewer than one hundred franchise outlets. Only 5 percent support five hundred or more units, and 7 percent are still looking for their first franchisee.

Many people find those numbers surprising, if not shocking. Most franchise companies never grow larger than one hundred units!

We also know that franchising as a methodology is used by businesses in seventy-five major industries, including quick-service restaurants (the largest sector), automotive repair, senior care, home services, construction, entertainment, financial services, etc. Some of the largest franchise companies are in the food and beverage industry, but some of the most successful franchise companies are in real estate, education, and business services, to name a few.

Get the Relevant Facts

Overall, franchising is best described as diverse. So how can anyone study the industry and report *relevant* data about success and failure to a prospective buyer? It's very difficult if not impossible to do. Even at their best, averages and national trends are interesting to read, but no one should use them to make a buying decision about a franchise.

If I told you that "most" franchises survive—a true statement—does that help you? There would still be "some" franchises that fail. You might think the odds are in your favor, and so while you're still a bit uncertain, you go ahead and invest your life savings in a franchise opportunity.

And two years later you're out of money and forced into bankruptcy. You can't understand it because, after all, "most" franchises survive.

Yes, they do, but you selected one that didn't. Assuming that you did everything right as a franchisee, it was just your "bad luck" that you selected the wrong franchise!

Or was it?

You can wrestle with the national data that the media report from time to time about franchising, or you can simply ignore it. Wise investors ignore it because it does not matter!

You Must Get this Part Right

But here's what you must not ignore: the success and/or failure history of the specific franchise brand you intend to buy!

That's a critical component of your due diligence. In fact, if you get this part right, you'll know whether or not you should buy a specific franchise opportunity, and you'll be confident about your decision.

Here's the good news: While it's unlikely that you can get specific data or scientific evidence, you can still determine the success or failure history of specific franchise opportunities. More than anything else you do, uncovering this information about specific franchise opportunities will take away your fear of franchising.

Once you get a franchisor's disclosure document, you can go to work to figure out the success versus failure history of that brand, and that's *relevant* data. It doesn't matter how *all* franchises perform across the board or within their industries. What matters is the performance of the *one* franchise opportunity that you hope to buy!

You may have to dig deep into a half dozen opportunities before you discover the right one to buy, based on the success-versus-failure history. But if you want to give yourself the best opportunity to succeed in franchising, there's no substitute for the work that needs to be done.

167

What Franchise Attorneys Say

Hoping to find a shortcut to this critical information—success versus failure—and to uncover a scientific methodology for capturing the data, I interviewed two seasoned franchise attorneys who frequently help clients perform due diligence on franchise opportunities.

Warren Lee Lewis (https://www.akerman.com/en/people/warren-lewis.html) is chair of the Franchise & Licensing Practice at Akerman LLP in Washington, D.C. He is also a member of the North American Securities Administrators Association (NASAA) (www.nasaa.org/about-us/) Franchise Project Group's Industry Advisory Committee. NASAA is responsible for facilitating compliance with franchise disclosure requirements under state franchise investment laws.

Cheryl L. Mullin (www.mullinlawpc.com) spearheads Mullin Law, PC in Richardson, Texas, a Dallas suburb, and was recognized in Best Lawyers in America®, Franchise Law, 2007-2017, and named to Texas Super Lawyers®, Franchise and Distribution Law, 2011-2016.

Both attorneys agreed that while there's no scientific methodology for determining the success-versus-failure rate of a franchise company—at least not without the cooperation of the franchisor and its franchisees and an independent auditor to examine the data provided—prospective franchisees can still take several specific steps to get a handle on a franchise brand's success-versus-failure history.

Grab the Disclosure Document

The first step is to get a copy of the franchisor's current disclosure document, which includes twenty-three items of information to help you decide if this is the right franchise opportunity for you. While an attorney most likely prepared the disclosure document for the franchisor, don't worry. The document must be written in simple English. If you can read and understand this book, you can read and understand most of a disclosure document's content.

Federal law requires franchisors to provide an annually updated disclosure document to prospective franchisees prior to selling a franchise in the United

States. Franchisors are not required to give a disclosure document to foreign investors, but many will do so simply because the disclosure document is the best way to explain a franchise opportunity.

A legitimate franchisor selling a franchise in the United States will not ask you to sign any binding documents or pay any money until you've had the disclosure document in your possession for a minimum of 14 days. You and your advisers, which may include an attorney, an accountant, and a franchise or business consultant, should use the contents of the disclosure document to help you form opinions and conclusions relative to the franchise opportunity.

Turn First to the Financial Statements

Lewis and Mullin both almost immediately turn to the franchisor's financial statements, Item 21, to get an advance idea of the franchisor's performance.

"I want to see whether revenues and profits are growing or declining," explains Mullin.

"I look at profit and loss," says Lewis, "to determine if it's really a company. And if it is a company, and it's making money, what's it doing with the money? Are they taking every dollar out of the business, or are they using the money to reinvest in the franchise system?"

Both attorneys pointed out that they carefully read the notes that pertain to the financial statements. "Sometimes there is good information in the notes," says Mullin. "For example, I just read a disclosure document where the franchisor said in Item 1 that it had no predecessors or affiliates in a similar business, but the notes to the financial statements talked about how the franchisor was a successor to some other company that was engaged in the same business."

For most of us, especially if we're not lawyers, it may seem tedious to read the notes at the end of a financial statement, but a good lawyer isn't going to gloss over any of the data in a disclosure document.

Charting a Franchisor's Performance

After examining Item 21, Item 20 (Outlets and Franchisee Information), also provides early indicators of a franchisor's value, and both attorneys say it's important to pay attention to this section. The data in Item 20 is fodder for helping you determine the success-versus-failure rate of the franchise brand. However, studying the information will take time, especially if you're new to franchise due diligence, and you may want to engage one or more of your advisers to help you make sense of the information.

There are five charts in Item 20 and each (with one exception), covers a three-year period

(1) System-Wide Outlet Summary—shows the number of outlets owned by franchisees and by the company (many franchisors do not own any outlets);

(2) Transfers of Outlets to New Owners—shows the exchange of ownership that occurs when a franchisee sells to a new franchisee;

(3) Status of Franchise Outlets—shows the number of outlets opened, terminated, non-renewed, reacquired by the franchisor, and ceased operations;

(4) Status of Company-Owned Outlets (if any); and,

(5) Projected New Franchised Outlets—shows the franchisor's growth projections by state.

Perhaps you quickly realized that Charts 2 and 3 are important indicators of a franchise brand's success-versus-failure rate. If the number of transfers is rapidly increasing, you'd want to know why. Is it because franchisees are failing? Not making enough money? Or are they unhappy with the franchisor?

If more franchise units are terminated than sold, or they're not renewed, or the franchisor is acquiring a large percentage of units every year, something's wrong with that franchise. These are all red flags that should prompt you to ask the franchisor for more information.

"You cannot use the data in these charts to get a percentage of success or failure," says Lewis, "but the charts reveal a snapshot of the franchise company. The data tells you if the system is growing or if there's been a lot of turnover of units, or if units are being terminated. In all cases, it's important to ask why. A lot of turnover may be occurring because the franchisees are not making money!"

Is There an Earning's Claim?

Item 19, Financial Performance Representations, is also an early indicator of success or failure, but only if the information is provided by the franchisor. This is the one optional item in the disclosure document. While franchisors are obligated to provide all other information required by the disclosure document, they do not have to file what's commonly called an "earning's claim." However, if they decide not to provide this information, they are prohibited from discussing earnings with a prospective franchisee.

Some franchisors, in fact, prefer not to discuss earnings, especially if they're unimpressive. So when you ask, "If I buy your franchise, how much money will I earn?" it's easier and safer for the franchisor to say, "I'm not permitted to disclose that information."

You might even hear a franchisor claim, "The law doesn't allow us to disclose earnings information," but that's not true. The law encourages franchisors to disclose earnings in Item 19 but does not force them to do so. Of course, critics of franchising think that's a bad idea, and franchisors should be forced to include financial performance representations, but at the moment, that's not the law.

"Most of the disclosure documents that I review disclose financial performance," explains Mullin. It's important to note "some are more detailed than others," she says. For example, some disclose only gross sales numbers, which is permitted by law.

But in that case, Lewis adds, where the franchisor discloses the top-line revenue produced by a franchisee but doesn't include the franchisee's costs, you don't know if the franchisee earns a profit. While it's not unusual for new businesses to operate in the red for a period of time, if the business doesn't eventually break even and begin to operate in the black, it's most likely going to fail.

Disclosure Items 19 (if it's included), 20, and 21 are indicators of the franchise brand's success-versus-failure history, and the information offered in these items will lead you to the next step in your franchise brand due diligence.

Here's the Gold Mine

In addition to the five charts, Item 20 includes contact information for current and former franchisees. *Voila!* This is your gold mine. If you'll work the gold mine, that's where you'll get the answers to all your questions, including, "Am I a good fit for this business?"

The Franchise Rule requires franchisors to provide contact information for their current franchisees. In addition, franchisors are required to provide contact information for every franchisee whose outlet was terminated, canceled, or not renewed, or the franchisee otherwise voluntarily or involuntarily ceased to do business under the franchise agreement during the most recently completed fiscal year.

These lists of current and former franchisees provide a neat database for you to continue exploring the success-versus-failure history of the franchise brand. All you've got to do is contact the franchisees and ask the appropriate questions!

In my best-selling book, *101 Questions to Ask Before You Invest in a Franchise* https://www.amazon.com/dp/B00EYT5BB6/?tag=hotobuafr-20) I provide a comprehensive list of questions to ask franchisees, franchisors, franchise advisers and even vendors to franchise companies. Several of those questions pertain to the success-versus-failure history of the franchise company while others pertain to the prospective franchisee's likelihood of succeeding in a given business.

Before contacting franchisees, it's a good idea to make a list of the dozen or so questions you want to ask and then make sure you ask each question of a dozen or so franchisees. If you track the answers in writing, you'll produce a document that eventually will help you make decisions with clarity. If you asked a dozen franchisees, "Given the opportunity, would you buy the same franchise all over again?" and ten of twelve said, "Absolutely," or something to that effect, it's going to be easier to know what you should do.

Don't Overlook Other Sources

While completing due diligence, it's not enough simply to interview franchisees. You can ask franchisors pertinent questions, too. For example: "What is the success rate of your franchisees?" . . . "Why would I buy your opportunity instead of your competitor's opportunity?" . . . "Where do you see this business ten years from now?" . . . "What's the profile of your most successful franchisees?"

Vendors also provide great insights about the success-versus-failure of the brands they serve. They not only may know how the franchisor performs financially, but they are likely to have pertinent information about the performance of specific franchisees to whom they sell products and/or services.

A vendor who provides cheese to a sandwich shop or pancake mix to a restaurant or cones to an ice cream parlor knows the volume of products sold by the franchisee. Vendors also know how the volume fluctuates, perhaps by seasons. They also know which franchisees pay their bills on time, which may or may not be an indicator of success or failure.

If you can locate vendors—and don't hesitate to ask the franchisor and franchisees for a vendor's contact information—don't be afraid to interview them. As much as they want to protect their customers, they also want to protect innocent people from business angst and catastrophes. Besides, they're not looking to take on new franchisee customers who aren't going to be able to pay their bills!

At a minimum, vendors can share with you pertinent information about territories, store locations, and other market factors that separate high-volume stores from low-volume stores.

Overall Best Source: Franchisees

But ultimately, some of the most valuable information you can gather about the franchise opportunity, and in particular the success-versus-failure history, will come from franchisees, current and past. That's why savvy franchise prospects use the Item 20 database to complete their due diligence.

You can expect the Item 20 information about existing franchisees to be current, but information about past franchisees is most likely out of date. Franchisors are not required to keep track of past franchisees or to update their contact information. Phone calls and emails to previous franchisees will most likely not be answered. Oftentimes, these former franchisees do not want to be found or they do not want to discuss their past relationship with a franchisor. In some cases, especially if the two parties disagreed and arrived at a settlement, in or out of court, the former franchisee is legally prevented from discussing the relationship.

Finding former franchisees and engaging them in meaningful conversation is a challenge.

However, it's easy to contact existing franchisees to get them to agree to speak with you by phone, answer your questions via email, and/or welcome a visit from you to give you time to observe their business for a day. Once you demonstrate to a franchisee that you're a serious candidate – that is, you've read the disclosure document, you qualify financially to buy the franchise, and you've attended the franchisor's Discovery Day (or plan to) – you'll find most franchisees to be helpful.

Franchisees Reserve Time for Serious Candidates

Franchisees are busy people and they don't want to spend time talking to "tire kickers" or people who are simply "dreaming" about buying a business but who have no idea of the expectations and requirements. They want to know that you've already done some homework. They're not obligated to talk to you, and they're not paid to talk to you (if they are, that information must be disclosed). Most franchisees are willing to give you their time and information because they share an *esprit de corps*. They want to be helpful. Besides, they may remember when they were in your shoes and they needed franchisees to help them.

Of course, franchisees also want to protect their brand. They want to be sure that you're not only qualified to buy a franchise, but that you're the type of person they would welcome into the franchise network.

You should expect that after talking to you or meeting you in person, the franchisees will report back to the franchisor to share their opinions, especially if they're unfavorable.

In some cases, however, where franchisees believe that another franchisee (or unit) in their territory would cut into their sales, it doesn't matter whether or not you're a good candidate. Those franchisees will campaign against you because they don't want additional competition. Ultimately, however, the franchisor is in control of deciding where and when to add franchise locations.

If you invest time getting to know franchisees, it's almost impossible not to find one or several who will take you into their confidence. They'll not only tell you the upside of buying and operating the franchise, but they'll tell you the downside, too.

Seasoned Franchisees are Most Helpful

You might discover franchisees who are members of the brand's franchise advisory council. Ask the franchisor for the names of those franchisees or ask existing franchisees to point you to them. In their role as advisers to the franchisor and representatives of the franchisees, they're usually comfortable talking about the pros and cons of the business and about the performance of specific franchisees. They're not intimidated by the franchisor—as some new franchisees may be—and if they've been franchisees for many years, they know the company's success-versus-failure history.

If past franchisee failures were the fault of under-capitalized or rogue franchisees, advisory council members are likely to tell you so. If past franchisee failures were the fault of the franchisor—perhaps selling a bad territory or encroaching on a franchisee's territory or falling short in the areas of training and support—they'll tell you that, too.

Other Pertinent Information

While I've emphasized Items 19, 20, and 21, all items in the disclosure document serve a valuable purpose and you need to study them to complete your due diligence.

For example, Items 5 through 7 address the fees you'll pay, including the upfront franchise fee, the ongoing royalty, and, if required, the advertising fund fee. This information details what it will cost you to operate the franchise. Franchise attorney Mullin says she looks at this data and compares it to the earnings potential of the franchise opportunity. "Does the initial investment make sense in light of the anticipated return on investment and the market challenges?" she asks.

Item 8 (Restrictions on Sources of Products and Services), tells you if you're free to buy from sources of your choice or if you must buy from sources owned by, or controlled by, the franchisor. You thought you'd buy the franchise and acquire materials or items for re-sale from your own family's business, or a friend's business, only to discover that's not permitted by the franchisor.

Item 16 (Restrictions on What the Franchisee May Sell), tells you exactly that, while Item 12 (Territory) addresses protected versus non-protected territories. Mullin says, "I look at territorial protections and restrictions. Can franchisees provide offsite services? Delivery and catering services? Sell on the Internet? The more freedom a franchisee has to go out and develop a territory, the more attractive" the franchise opportunity may be. But some franchisors restrict the franchisee to operate in a specific location while keeping other revenue streams for the franchisor's benefit.

Both Mullin and Lewis urge you to consider Item 3 (Litigation) and Item 4 (Bankruptcy) to determine the experience of the people who own the franchise company. "What kind of people are they?" asks Lewis.

Keep in mind that you need to go through this process for each franchise opportunity that you'd seriously consider buying, and the process may take you a couple of weeks to a couple of months to complete. It's a mistake not to complete due diligence for each brand even though if you're seriously considering three or four brands you may spend six to eight months doing little more than conducting due diligence.

Bottom line: By following the guidelines in this chapter, you can uncover the success-versus-failure history of any franchise opportunity and in doing so give yourself the pertinent information you need to make a "buy" or "not buy" decision.

And that's how you take the fear out of franchising!

Funding Your Franchise Acquisition:
Where Do You Get the Money?

Two common mistakes that prospective franchisees make when they're exploring franchise opportunities are (1) ignorance of their personal financial status and capabilities; and (2) ignorance of the financial requirements to buy a franchise.

Do you know your credit score and how much cash you can invest in a franchise, or bring to the table to leverage additional funds? Do you know what banks, leasing companies, the U.S. Small Business Administration, and special funds designated for franchise lending will require of you to secure a loan?

The sooner you get on top of these issues, the better—otherwise, you may be wasting your time. You should expect franchisors, and franchise brokers, to ask you these questions even before they give you a Franchise Disclosure Document. Not to do so could mean the franchisor is wasting his or her time because you may not be able to acquire the franchise.

Good News for Borrowers

If you need to borrow money to acquire a franchise, the good news is that lenders are looking for good deals to fund. While there's still not a national lender for franchise opportunities, as existed prior to 2008, nowadays more community banks lend to franchisees, more franchisors lend to franchisees, several franchise-specific funds underwrite franchise acquisitions, and for those who have a retirement fund, the fund can be rolled into seed money to capitalize a business.

According to Robert Coleman, who publishes the Coleman Report (www.colemanreport.com), lenders view franchises as "a little bit better risk than mom-and-pop businesses," but they favor established brands and experienced franchisees. "If you've been successfully operating a unit for several years and now you need money to open another one to three units, you can get that money," says Coleman. You can get the money to open your first unit, too, but it will take a little more scrutiny.

FRANdata, the franchise information firm based outside of Washington, D.C., reported that franchising is now growing at its fastest rate in five years, largely because prospective and existing franchisees have been able to find money.

How Do You Get a Loan Today?

So what's it going to take today to get the money you need to acquire a franchise opportunity?

Business financing expert Doug Smith of Biz Finance Solutions in Colorado (www.BizFinanceSolutions.com) explains that there are two types of funding: equity-based and debt-based.

"Using the money you have in your retirement plan, rolling it over without penalty or taxation, and using it as an injection to get a U.S. government-backed loan, is equity financing," he says, and it's an option that many franchisees use today.

"Debt-based funding requires a credit score and credit history to get a conventional bank loan or unsecured business financing, including equipment leasing, and unsecured personal loans. But if your credit score is weak, or you've filed a bankruptcy, it's the kiss of death."

Your personal financial situation, and your thoughts about financial risk, may determine how you should proceed when you seek financing.

The 401(k) Rollover

Smith's preferred franchise funding strategy is the 401(k) Rollover (www.invest-faq.com/articles/ret-plan-401k.html), and most people don't seem to know about it. Or, if they do, they've been told it's illegal or dangerous. However, this option has the blessing of the U.S. government, and here are the facts you need to know:

If you have a retirement fund and you change employers, you have three important options:

179

1. Leave the fund where it is…the majority of people choose this option.

2. Move the fund into a new account, such as a self-directed IRA.

3. Move the fund to your new employer's 401(k), thus consolidating your retirement savings in one fund.

Most people aren't aware of Option #3, beginning with becoming your own employer!

That is, you can become a franchisee and establish a C Corporation with stock and a 401(k). Becoming your own employer puts you in the enviable position of self-funding your own business, tax-free! You can move—or what the Internal Revenue Service refers to as rollover—your existing retirement money into your new employer's 401(k), and the cash can be used to buy and operate a franchise. It's tax-free, penalty-free (if done correctly), legal, and may be your best option for funding your business, particularly if you don't have other resources, or you can't qualify for a traditional loan.

Isn't This Controversial?

The U.S. Internal Revenue Service and the Department of Labor have established guidelines and directives for implementing a 401(k) Rollover. You can't use the rollover to dodge taxes, or to personally benefit from the money. Some years ago a financial broker was shut down for a period of time for stretching the rules, and that incident gave rise to the notion that the rollover is illegal. It's not. If you use the rollover for the right reasons—you can't use it for a scheme; it has to be used with a real business—you (or your adviser) set it up correctly and comply annually with the regulations, you should be able to avoid any objections or complications. Follow the spirit of the guidelines with appropriate intentions and you should remain in the clear.

Of course, the IRS reserves the right to change the rules, and that's why it's extremely important that you work with a credible company, or broker, that has a track record for successfully implementing and maintaining rollovers.

Two Benefits of a 401(k) Rollover

The 401(k) Rollover has made a good name for itself among franchisors, who frequently recommend the strategy to prospective franchisees. Here are two reasons why:

- If the franchise acquisition is a small investment—under $150,000—franchisors know that lenders aren't attracted to small loans. There's no money to be made processing small loans, so lenders avoid them. That makes a rollover more attractive. Rollover money can be used to pay for the franchise fee and to buy equipment. When you don't have collateral, or you're buying a business that provides a service from your home, a vehicle, or a small office, the 401(k) Rollover may be your best choice for funding your business.

- After a rollover, you can use the cash as equity to qualify for a conventional or SBA-guaranteed loan. You'll likely need a cash injection of 30 percent to secure a loan. In the past, borrowers used equity in real estate, i.e., their personal residence, to qualify for a loan. Now you can use rollover money for your cash injection.

"People who utilize a rollover are more successful in the average business," reveals Geoff Seiber, president and CEO of FranFund in Fort Worth, Texas (FranFund.com). "People who use this strategy tend to stay in business longer because they used their retirement money to fund their business and they don't have debt to service."

Can You Accept the Risks?

Used properly, the 401(k) Rollover is an aggressive way to capitalize your business. The challenge, however, is that by using it you give up the security of a retirement fund. Some people can't handle that emotionally. *Can you?* Will you feel comfortable knowing that your retirement money is now invested in your own business? If not, you probably don't want to use this funding strategy. On the other hand, people who start businesses, and plan to operate them, aren't usually looking for comfort.

In the U.S., numerous companies provide rollover services, including: Biz Finance Solutions, Guidant, FranFund, and Benetrends. Expect to spend in the range of $5,000 with one of these firms to set up your rollover. The firm will also offer to provide necessary administrative services to keep your fund in check, and that may cost you in the range of $100 monthly.

It's important to keep your rollover plan in compliance with the laws because the IRS audits these plans. "Under 2 percent of our plans are audited every year," says Seiber, "which is the norm in our industry. By not doing the administrative work properly, you're taking a bigger risk" if the IRS audits your account.

Options to the 401(k) Rollover

Unless you have a pile of cash that you intend to inject into your deal, i.e., a retirement fund that you will rollover or savings that you will bring to the table, your funding options are severely limited. It's even worse if you're a new franchisee and you want to buy a single unit—an existing franchisee with plans to expand, or a multi-unit operator, will find more options.

Look to Your Franchisor for Funding

Guys like Coleman, Smith, and Seiber are among a select corps of experts who can advise prospective franchisees when they need financing, but there's only so much they can do in a reticent financial market. If you can't take advantage of the programs they offer or recommend, your best source of funding may be your franchisor of choice. If you know that you will need money to acquire a franchise, look for franchisors who lend to franchisees. Even franchisors who don't loan money to franchisees know the lenders who will, so ask your finance-related questions early in your franchise exploration.

And don't give up! Some of the most successful franchisees today started out by investing in a low-cost franchise and expanding when they could afford to do so. Many others started out with money borrowed from family and friends. If franchising makes sense for you, you'll find a franchise company that will help you clear the lending hurdles.

Here's One More Funding Option: VetFran®

VetFran, sponsored by the International Franchise Association (IFA), helps veterans of the U.S. armed services buy franchise opportunities by providing financial assistance, training, and industry support.

VetFran was created by the late Don Dwyer Sr.—founder of The Dwyer Group, a conglomerate of franchise companies, to say "thank you" to America's veterans returning from the first Gulf War. After the Sept. 11, 2001, terrorist attacks, IFA re-launched VetFran and the program continues to this day.

Nearly six hundred franchise brands voluntarily offer financial incentives and mentoring to prospective franchisees who are veterans. Thousands of veterans have utilized VetFran to buy franchises. If you're a veteran, be sure to ask your franchisor of choice, "Do you support VetFran?" This may be an additional source of funding for you.

Foreign Investors:
Use Franchising to Get Your U.S. Green Card

F ranchising has recently become a fast-track opportunity for foreign investors who want to move to the United States. Thousands of foreign investors have already taken advantage of the Immigrant Investor Program administered by the U.S. Citizenship and Immigration Services (USCIS), and the number of applicants is rising dramatically in part due to favorable changes in the program, and in part due to franchising.

Known as EB-5, the program was created to stimulate the U.S. economy through job creation and capital investment by foreign investors. Essentially, a qualified foreigner invests $500,000 to $1 million directly into a business, such as any of the 12 amazing franchise opportunities in this book, or into a regional fund that invests in businesses, and gets a green card and eventually U.S. citizenship, providing that the investment created at least ten full-time jobs for at least two years.

You Can Move Your Family to the U.S.

Foreign investors are using EB-5 to move their families to the U.S., or to send their children to the U.S. to study. A married investor, for example, gets visas for himself, his spouse, and all unmarried children under the age of 21. While the program has been slow to get off the ground—it has existed since 1990—more than $4 billion was invested in 2013 alone, and interest has spiked in part due to franchising.

Look around the U.S. and you'll find foreigners operating many franchised businesses. Of course, America exists because of industrious foreigners, and franchisors welcome them because they are enthusiastic about learning a successful operating system that they and their family members can use to change their lives for the better. However, EB-5 does not require investors to actually work in a business; after investing their money, foreign investors can live wherever they choose, start their own business, take a job, or retire!

A Means for U.S. Expansion

Any U.S. franchisor today who isn't aware of EB-5 is missing a huge opportunity for expansion. Many American franchisors are focused on international expansion—they want to sell master licenses to foreigners who will build out the franchise brand in their own countries—but EB-5 provides an opportunity to build more franchises in the U.S. with foreign capital and expertise. While many franchise companies are unaware of this opportunity, that will soon change because franchising is a small community and news travels fast.

What's the Red Tape?

Of course, as with any bureaucratic program, there are numerous requirements and regulations with EB-5, and it's not simply a matter of popping half-a-million dollars or more into a franchisor's bank account on Friday afternoon and moving the family to the U.S. during the weekend. The investor must prove his or her money came from a lawful source, and must also pass the scrutiny of U.S. immigration investors. The U.S. is for sale, but not to criminals and terrorists.

In addition, the investment must create tangible employment: at least ten permanent, full-time jobs for two years. However, indirect or induced jobs count, and that's where franchising holds the trump card.

A Match for Franchising

Originally, most of the EB-5 money was invested into real estate projects that may or may not have created the requisite employment. But $500,000 invested into certain franchised businesses (in rural environments) or $1 million (in urban environments) can create upwards of forty jobs, including induced jobs that result from the supply chain.

Consider what happens when a franchisor sells a new franchise. There are direct jobs—created for the franchisee and others who work within the business—and indirect jobs—created in the supply chain. For example, when Xpresso Delight opens a new franchise, the business creates jobs for salespeople (who place coffee machines in offices) and support staff (who maintain the machines and build rapport with customers). But the business also creates jobs in the supply chain for people who manufacture the coffee machines, grow the coffee beans, manufacture paper products, such as cups, and so on. Plus there are jobs for payroll clerks, administrative assistants, and other support staff. USCIS takes all of those jobs into account to qualify an investor.

Multi-Unit Operators to Benefit

If an investor doesn't want to be a franchisee, he doesn't have to be. Again, franchising is perfect for this program. In many franchise networks, there are multi-unit operators, or would-be multi-unit operators, who seek expansion capital, and sometimes partners. And once again, most of these operators have never heard of EB-5, but they will (through books such as this, through media, and through their franchise networks), and they'll want to know how to find these investors.

Timing is everything, and in the case of EB-5 and franchising, now is the time. However, this program takes times—from the moment an investor learns of the program, finds an investment vehicle, i.e., a franchise opportunity, or a regional center, and completes the USCIS documentation, six months to a year may pass. But to many investors, that's a very short time and a small price to pay to gain access to life in the United States.

The USCIS website (www.uscis.gov/working-united-states/permanent-workers/employment-based-immigration-fifth-preference-eb-5/about-eb-5-visa-classification) is a good place to learn more about this program.

How to Succeed with a Franchise Broker
By Jason Killough, CFE

Do you want to own a franchise but don't have the foggiest idea where to start? Wouldn't it be nice to have an expert, at no cost to you, walk you through the process? A franchise broker, or franchise consultant, may be the authority you're looking for to move you through the franchise vetting-and-purchasing process, from start to finish.

With several thousand franchises in at least 200 industries, a potential candidate wading through franchise information on the Internet is likely to get lost, if they even know where to begin. All of that guesswork and legwork is taken out of the equation when a seasoned franchise broker enters the picture.

A franchise broker serves as the go-between for potential franchisees and franchisors, who pay brokers to find a good fit for their franchises. The broker's goal to both future franchisees and franchisors is to create a win-win relationship. If the potential candidate buys a franchise, the parent company pays the broker a fee.

Brokers are charged with finding candidates who will be the most successful (i.e., top royalty generators) in their franchise networks. By doing so, this produces the pure, win-win nature of the relationship where all interests are aligned and transparent. If someone becomes a top royalty generator, it (by definition) means they are successful and, thus, everyone in the equation is happy.

So how do you find such a valuable adviser? Start by looking for a seasoned broker who has worked extensively with franchises. It helps if the broker is a Certified Franchise Executive, a designation awarded by the International Franchise Association.

The best brokers have worked in franchising for more than 20 years, they understand how franchising works, and they only agree to work on behalf of leading, high-potential franchise brands.

Experienced brokers have seen every possible scenario when it comes to finding and buying the right franchise. Brokers are an essential franchise-

exploring "value-add" as they share their expertise in all aspects of buying a franchise.

Building Blocks and Rapport

Early in your relationship with a franchise broker, the broker will review your background and discuss your goals as they pertain to owning a franchise. The broker will likely want to know:

- Where you grew up, your family dynamic
- Education
- Career background
- Which industries pique your interest
- How much capital you have to invest
- What's important to you
- Where you want to own a franchise
- Why you want to own a franchise
- How soon you plan to make a decision

In other words, the broker wants to get to know you, and what's important to you. This will help the broker think about potential franchise opportunities that will meet your requirements.

Are You Right for a Franchise?

With those foundation blocks firmly in place, many franchise brokers will assess your potential as a franchisee. Some brokers will use profiling instruments and other meta-analysis profiling tools such as e-Quiz.net, DiSC, or another proprietary tool.

Profiling helps brokers determine first and foremost if buying a franchise makes sense for you, and if so, the type of franchise you should buy. If a broker doesn't assess your talents, skills, and behaviors, you might think about looking for another broker. Keep in mind, the broker's services are free to you.

With results from a profiling tool, you'll have a better idea of whether purchasing a franchise makes sense. Maybe you should keep your job, or look for a different job. Why move forward into franchising if you're more suited for another career option? Buying a franchise will likely require you to make a significant financial decision. Get all the input you can to make the best decision. For starters, make sure you're compatible with franchising.

If your personality and work habits are a good fit for franchising, a broker will then begin to narrow down the type of franchises to put on your short list. Brokers represent hundreds of different franchise opportunities, but it doesn't make sense to introduce you to food franchises, for example, or retail-based franchises if you're not suited for these types of businesses.

At this point, the broker will likely delve into:

- Where do you want your franchise to be located?
- Do you want to work from home, an office, a storefront, or in a mobile/truck-based franchise?
- Are you interested in retail or fast food, business-to-business or business-to-consumer opportunities?
- What are your concerns?
- Why will you be a good fit for a certain type of franchise?
- What do you have to offer to the franchisor?
- Why should the franchisor select you from among other candidates?
- What are your assets, liabilities, and net worth?
- Do you have sufficient liquidity for investing in a franchise

Finding a Right-fit Franchise

Once your broker has answers to this long list of questions, he or she searches for potential franchise brands (checking their available territories) that should fit your requirements. After introducing you to the franchise brands that interest you, your broker can also put you in touch with franchise attorneys, real estate contacts, potential lenders, and other valuable resources.

The broker may eventually give you a list of potential franchise opportunities and invite you to begin researching the brands. You can usually begin this process by visiting the franchisors' websites.

After you complete your initial research, the broker will ask you to evaluate the brands to indicate your preferences, if any. If you find one or more brands that really interest you, the broker will contact the companies directly on your behalf and make an introduction for you.

Spend Time Doing Due Diligence

Now it's time to get to know the franchisor and its franchisees. Your franchise broker might give you a checklist to help you begin this process, but ultimately you'll need to do your own due diligence. The broker won't do the due diligence for you, and you should reject a broker who suggests doing so. This is your investment and it must be based on your own research and investigation.

If your preliminary investigation is favorable, and the franchisor likes your background and profile, you'll be offered the Franchise Disclosure Document (FDD). It's free and does not obligate you in any way. It's the tool you need to conduct the balance of your due diligence (see the chapter titled: How to Investigate Before You Invest in a Franchise).

The FDD provides intimate details about a franchise opportunity. Working with your broker, it will be easier for you to discuss the significance with someone who knows a great deal about franchising.

If you're serious about taking the franchise leap, consider working with a qualified franchise broker.

Jason Killough, CFE, is a member of the The Entrepreneur Authority (TEA) franchise broker network (eAuth.com). He works with candidates across the U.S. and can be reached at jkillough@eAuth.com or by calling 1-800-390-FRAN.

Franchise Terms and Resources

The following lists provide information about franchising, including resources that may help you while you're pursuing a franchise opportunity. Please keep in mind that the inclusion of any resource does not imply the author's endorsement. The information in these lists is not exhaustive. If you're looking for something that you can't find in this section, please visit www.howtobuyafranchise.com and use our Contact form.

Franchise Terms

Here are some of the most common terms used in franchising.

Advertising Co-op

A participatory body of franchisees – occasionally including the franchisor – that contributes money to a common fund to pay for regional or national advertising programs.

Advertising Fee

Many franchise opportunities require franchisees to pay a monthly fee into an Advertising or Marketing Fund. The fee is generally represented as a percentage (for example, 2 percent) and is almost always calculated on the franchisee's gross sales, as opposed to net sales or profits. The Advertising Fee may also be a flat fee. The Advertising Fee is ongoing and will be collected while the franchise agreement is in effect. Advertising Fund monies are used to advertise the franchise brand, its products and/or services. This is not money to be used by the franchisor!

Ad Fund

Franchisees pay their Advertising Fees into an Ad Fund, which is used to underwrite the cost of advertising and promotions for franchisees. The franchisor, or Franchise Advisory Council, establishes the Ad Fund and oversees it on behalf of franchisees. Ad Fund money is often used to hire advertising and marketing agencies to assist the franchise network.

Angel Investor

An individual or group of individuals who provide capital for a business start-up, usually in exchange for convertible debt or ownership equity.

Area Developer

The franchisor awards a single franchisee the right to operate more than one unit within a definied area, under a development agreement and based on an agreed-upon development schedule.

Business Valuation

The practice of valuing an existing business.

Buy-back Option

A term of the franchise agreement wherein if the franchisee goes out of business, the franchisor retains the right to buy back all assets at a pre-agreed price.

Conversion Franchising

The process by which existing independent businesses or dealers within an industry become franchisees when they assume the trade name and trade dress of the franchisor.

Disclosure

In some countries, and especially in the United States, franchisors are *required* by federal and some state laws to "disclose" individuals who are serious about acquiring a franchise. Disclosure is a process that includes providing prospective franchisees with a copy of the franchisor's Franchise Disclosure Document (FDD) and Franchise Agreement. The FDD must be delivered to a franchise candidate at least fourteen days prior to the candidate purchasing the franchise. Disclosure minimizes fraudulent sales in franchising and promotes the safety and longevity of franchising. Franchisors are required to comply with specific disclosure regulations that disseminate helpful information to prospective franchisees in advance of paying any money or signing any documents.

Disclosure Document

See Franchise Disclosure Document.

Discovery Day

An event set up by the franchisor so that potential franchisees may learn more about become a franchisee. Discovery day typically takes place at the franchisors HQ and is often the final step in the due diligence process. It provides the opportunity to meet the management/support teams and trainers face-to-face.

Earning's Claim

An Earning's Claim (or a Financial Performance Representation) may be included in a franchisor's Franchise Disclosure Document. An Earning's Claim documents the earnings of franchisees in the franchisor's network. *Most franchisors do not include Earning's Claims in their documents.* Those who do not are prohibited from making any oral or written statements concerning the actual or potential sales, costs, income, or profits of their franchise opportunities.

Equity Interest

Any legal ownership of the franchise business or the corporation that owns the franchise business.

Franchise

It's a license that grants an individual or an entity (i.e., a corporation) the right to use a franchisor's operating system for the purpose of marketing, selling, and distributing the franchisor's products and/or services. A franchise is a license.

Franchise Agreement

A legal document (license) signed by both the franchisor and the franchisee granting the franchisee the right to operate the franchise system for a specified period of time, in a specified format, and sometimes in a specified location. It's the legally binding document between franchisor and franchisee.

Franchise Associations

There are approximately forty trade associations throughout the world that represent the interests of franchisors and franchisees. See International Franchise Association.

Franchise Disclosure Document

Every franchisor in the United States is required to complete and maintain a Franchise Disclosure Document (FDD). The FDD, in layperson's language, describes the franchise opportunity. The items of disclosure are standard for all franchise companies. There are 23 Items that require disclosure, including Litigation, Initial Franchise Fee, Franchisee's Obligations, Franchisor's Obligations, Territory, Restrictions On What The Franchisee May Sell, Renewal, Termination, Transfer and Dispute Resolution, List of Outlets (Franchisees), Financial Statements, and more. Prospective franchisees should read the FDD several times before investing in the franchise.

Franchisee

The individual or entity (i.e., a corporation) that's assigned the rights to a franchise by a franchisor.

Franchise Expo

Franchise companies come together under one roof to exhibit their franchise opportunities for a day or more. The public is invited to these events. Expos sometimes include educational programs.

Franchise Fee

A one-time, upfront fee required by the franchisor. It must be disclosed in the Franchise Disclosure Document.

Franchise Portal

A website that promotes franchise opportunities and may also include educational information about franchising. The best example: FranchiseExpo.com.

Franchisor

The company that grants franchises to franchisees. The franchisor controls and owns the franchise system.

International Franchise Association

IFA is the world's largest trade organization representing both franchisors and franchisees. Headquarters: Washington, D.C.
Website: www.franchise.org.

International Franchise Expo

The world's premier event among franchise expos is sponsored by the International Franchise Association. The producer of the IFE is MFVExpositions. Website: www.ifeinfo.com.

Liquid Capital

Assets held in cash or in something that can be readily turned into cash. Also knows as "liquid assets".

Master Franchisee

A system whereby a franchisor grants to a party the right to operate franchised businesses and to grant sub-franchises to third parties, within an agreed-upon geographic area. The master franchisee typically retains a portion of the royalty as compensation for its services.

Multiunit Franchisee

A franchisee that owns and operates more than one franchised location.

Product Distribution Franchisee

A franchise where the franchisee simply sells the franchisor's products without using the franchisor's method of conducting business.

Royalty Fee

A payment by the franchisee to the franchisor. Usually represented as a percentage (as an example, 6 percent) and paid weekly or monthly. May also be a flat weekly or monthly fee. Royalties are almost always paid on the franchisee's gross sales, as opposed to net sales or profits. This is an ongoing fee that must be paid during the period of time the franchise agreement/license is in effect. The royalty fee must be disclosed in the Franchise Disclosure Document.

Site Selection

The process of choosing the location for a franchised business. Involves knowledge of demographics, traffic patterns, buying habits, market characteristics, wage/employment patterns, zoning and other land use regulations, building/health code ordinances, and real estate patterns.

Trademark

The marks, brand name and logo that identify a franchisor which is licensed to the franchisee.

Turnkey Operation

A term used to describe a franchise that is thoroughly organized, full equipped and professionally set up that the new franchisee need only "turn the key" in order to commence business.

Venture Capital

A person or group of individuals who invest in a business venture, providing capital for start-up or expansion. Venture capitalists are looking for a higher rate of return than would be given by more traditional investments.

Franchise Resources

Franchise Associations

International Franchise Association

1900 K St., NW, Suite 700

Washington, DC 20006

Phone: 202-628-8000

Website: www.franchise.org

In addition to representing franchisors and franchisees, the IFA also represents the Council of Franchise Suppliers, which includes attorneys, accountants, consultants, franchise brokers, and others who may be able to assist you in your exploration of franchising. IFA promotes numerous books and other resources about franchising and publishes *Franchising World* magazine. Free resources are included on the IFA's website.

Canadian Franchise Association

5399 Eglinton Ave. West, Suite 116

Toronto, Ontario

Canada M9C 5K6

Telephone: 416-695-2896

Email: info@cfa.ca

Website: www.cfa.ca

For a list of Franchise Associations Worldwide:

http://www.franchise.org

Franchise Expositions

MFV Expositions

Telephone: 201-226-1130

Website: www.mfvexpo.com

In addition to the International Franchise Expo, MFV Expositions produces regional franchise expos in cities such as Dallas, Los Angeles, and Chicago. MFV also produces international franchise events, including the London Franchise Expo and *Feria Internacional de Franquicias* in Mexico City.

U.S. Government Resources

U.S. Small Business Administration: http://www.sba.gov

U.S. Commerce Department International Trade Administration: www.ita.doc.gov

Books, Periodicals & Portals

7 Dirty Little Secrets of Franchising: Protect Your Franchise Investment, Amazon.com

12 Amazing Franchise Opportunities for 2015, Amazon.com

101 Questions to Ask Before You Invest in a Franchise, Amazon.com

Bond's Franchise Guide, Amazon.com

Buy 'Hot' Franchises Without Getting Burned, Amazon.com

Entrepreneur, www.entrepreneur.com, publishes the Franchise 500 every January

Franchise Handbook, www.franchisehandbook.com

FranchiseExpo.com, www.franchiseexpo.com

FranchiseGator.com, www.franchisegator.com

Franchise Opportunities Guide, www.franchise.org

Franchise Times, www.franchisetimes.com

Franchise Update, www.franchise-update.com

Franchising World, www.franchise.org

About The Author, Dr. John P. Hayes

John P. Hayes, Ph.D., began working in the franchise community in 1979 as a freelance writer. He continues to write about franchising for media worldwide, including newspapers, magazines, and books. On several occasions he has been a franchisee, and for several years he served as the President and CEO of one of America's major franchise companies, HomeVestors of America, Inc. He is one of the few people to have been a franchisee, a franchisor, and an adviser to franchisors and franchisees.

For many years, John's client list included the International Franchise Association (IFA), the International Franchise Expo (IFE), and dozens of franchise companies. For several years he toured the U.S. as part of IFA's regional training faculty, and on many occasions he has been a speaker and trainer for IFA, the IFE, and countless franchise companies. For several years starting in 1989, he traveled with the IFA's international franchise trade missions, marketing U.S. franchise opportunities in Europe, South America, the Pacific Rim, and the Far East.

John is a frequent speaker at international franchise expos, and a guest on radio and television to discuss franchise topics. He was featured in a thirty-minute television infomercial called *The Power of Franchising*. Through the years he has assisted franchisors and franchisees internationally to sell or acquire master licensing rights. For nearly thirty years, he has taught the most popular symposium at the International Franchise Expo: "The A to Zs of Buying a Franchise."

He is the co-author of *Franchising: The Inside Story* (with the late franchisor John Kinch); *You Can't Teach a Kid to Ride a Bike at a Seminar* (with the late franchisor David Sandler); *Start Small, Finish Big, 15 Lessons to Start & Operate Your Own Business*, (with the co-founder of Subway); and *Network Marketing for Dummies* (with the late Zig Ziglar).

In 2017, Palm Beach Atlantic University in West Palm Beach, Florida, created the Titus Center for Franchising and appointed John as the Titus Chair for Franchise Leadership. He teaches a franchise curriculum leading to a concentration in franchising for students of the Rinker School of Business at PBA. John formerly taught marketing and journalism at Gulf University for Science & Technology in Kuwait; he was a communications professor at Temple University where he was head of the Magazine Writing Sequence; and he taught journalism at Kent State University.

BizComPress

Do you have a story to tell that will help others improve their life, their business, or otherwise make a difference? BizCom Press can help you reach the widest audience possible. Founded by authors for authors, BizCom Press is a new kind of publishing company. Our award-winning team will help you write your book, edit it, design it, publish it, and promote it. And you keep the majority of your earnings!

Whether you already have a manuscript, or just the seed of an idea, contact us and we'll provide honest feedback based on decades of experience in book publishing. If we believe the manuscript or the idea has a market, we can develop a plan that fits your budget and you'll be on your way to becoming a published author.

For more information, contact Scott White at 214-458-5751 or Scott@BizComPress.com.

Let Me Know If You Buy A Franchise!

If this book was helpful in your decision to buy a franchise, please let me know by sending me an e-mail at john@bizcompress.com.

In return, I'll send you a FREE copy of my report

*"What franchisees must do to
succeed in first 90 days of operation!"*

which normally sells for $99.

— Dr. John P Hayes

Made in the USA
Middletown, DE
20 December 2018